The Perfect Hire

The Perfect Hire

A Tactical Guide to Hiring, Developing, and Retaining Top Sales Talent

Katherine Graham-Leviss
XBInsight, Inc.

Entrepreneur. Press

Publisher: Jere Calmes
Cover Design: Andrew Welyczko, CWL Publishing Enterprises, Inc.
Editorial and Production Services: CWL Publishing Enterprises, Inc., Madison, Wisconsin, www.cwlpub.com

This publication is designed to provide accurate and authoritative information in regard to the subject matter covered. It is sold with the understanding that the publisher is not engaged in rendering legal, accounting, or other professional services. If legal advice or other expert assistance is required, the services of a competent professional person should be sought.
> —From a Declaration of Principles jointly adopted by a
> Committee of the American Bar Association and
> a Committee of Publishers and Associations

ISBN 13: 978-1-59918-421-0
      10: 1-59918-421-4

Library of Congress Cataloging-in-Publication Data

Graham Leviss, Katherine.
   The perfect hire : a tactical guide to hiring, developing, and retaining top sales talent / by Katherine Graham-Leviss.
      p. cm.
   ISBN-13: 978-1-59918-421-0
   ISBN-10: 1-59918-421-4 (alk. paper)
      1. Sales management. 2. Sales management—Case studies.
   3. Selling. 4. Selling—Case studies. I. Title.
   HF5438.4.G715 2011
   658.3'044—dc23

                              2011025145

Every effort has been made to ensure that the information in this book is accurate and current at the time of publication. However, laws, regulations, policies, contact information, and so on may be changed without notice. This book is not a substitute for individual advice rendered by a professional who is able to work with you one-on-one.

15 14 13   10 9 8 7 6 5 4 3 2

Contents

Preface:
The Challenge

The task of the leader is to get his people from where they are to where they have not been.

—Henry Kissinger

MANY INDUSTRIES DEALING WITH THE CHALLENGE OF FINDING THE RIGHT SALES-people. We have all had the experience of hiring people for their background and technical skills and firing people for having a bad attitude. The lesson from this is that background and technical skills are not enough. You also need to define and access soft skills and the ability to solve problems in your potential hires.

The five steps outlined in this book, along with the supporting tools and information, give you a process for a powerful way to identify and hire the best candidates for any sales position you're looking to fill. It also shows you how to develop and retain your top salespeople once you find them.

Here's a brief overview of what this book covers:

Chapter 1, Making Informed Decisions. Helps anyone understand the importance of using a well-vetted process for hiring—one that will help you not only select the right candidate, but also create an environment that will develop and train your new sales talent.

Chapter 2, Step 1: Define the Job. Demonstrates a simple process that you can use to define each job you are seeking to fill. You can only attract the right fit when you have a clearly defined position. Many times someone in the company dusts off an old job description that could span a range of positions. This chapter provides the direction to develop a customized description that will attract top sales performers.

Chapter 3, Step 2: Benchmark the Job. Introduces assessments for hiring and explains how benchmarking will increase the accuracy of your job definition and match the best candidates to the job. The one way to be sure you'll hire high-performing salespeople is to identify the soft skills and problem-solving skills that are most important to the job and determine at what level they are performed by those who are successful on the job. Benchmarking the job will give you those insights.

Chapter 4, Assessing the 3 Cs: Competencies, Cognitive Abilities and Core Values. Provides insight into the areas that will give you the best predictors of on-the-job success for your final candidates.

Chapter 5, Step 3: Screen and Interview. Provides insight into being a hiring-ready company with a pool of candidates; then discusses the best practices for screening and interviewing.

Chapter 6, Step 4: Assess Your Top Candidates. Provides the detail you need to match assessments to their appropriate uses and to see just how many applications there are for the results. A case study shows how using the results for competencies, critical thinking, and values can help to guide hiring decisions.

Chapter 7, Case Study: Comparing Multiple Candidates. Shows how using assessments can make it easy to compare your top candidates' results to support your hiring decisions.

Chapter 8, Step 5: Develop Your Sales Talent. Provides the how-to and shows why hiring isn't complete until the new hire has a development plan that's part of the organizational ongoing development process.

Chapter 9, Case Study: Sales Team Analysis. Shows how using assessments to analyze the current sales team will give greater insights into any gaps that exist and how managers can develop their sales team to its full potential by addressing the team strengths as well as individual strengths and areas for improvement.

Chapter 10, Assessing Behaviors and Thinking Skills. Provides insight into using assessments to understand, develop, and manage employees.

Chapter 11, Retain Your Top Talent. Goes beyond development. This chapter shows how understanding the attributes you discover through hiring and development assessments can better position managers to adapt the work environment to best support your sales top performers.

ACKNOWLEDGMENTS

To my husband, Evan, for his thoughtful advice—no matter what time of day. For his support and inspiration through each year that XBInsight has grown. For his infinite patience when listening in that mindful, respectful, honest way I treasure.

To my son, Ethan, 9, who gives me such energy, with his compassion, deep thinking, and unique way of seeing the world.

To my son Hunter, 5 years old, who keeps me alert and appreciative, with his astounding attentiveness to everything around him and confidence to know what he wants.

To my son Cole, 5 years old, for his charm and humor, kindness and empathy, who always makes me smile, with his endearing hugs, sweet, loving words, and genuine sensitivity.

To Rick Crawshaw and MaryEllen Towle, who are exceptional coaches, for their high integrity and values, for their many years of service growing with the business, embracing new tools, helping me evolve to the innovative company XBInsight has become.

To Cindy Fox, an exceptional director of training, for her passion in representing the XC InSight System and tireless willingness to take on whatever project I put in front of her.

To all my clients for their commitment, support, and inspiration.

Chapter

1 Getting Good Recruits

I am convinced that nothing we do is more important than hiring and developing people. At the end of the day you bet on people, not on strategies.

—Larry Bossidy, Coauthor
Execution: The Discipline of Getting Things Done

CHOOSING THE RIGHT PEOPLE WHEN GROWING A HIGH-PERFORMING, PROFITABLE sales force is a significant challenge. When it's done well, the gains are considerable, because in our people lie most of our dollars. By selecting employees who have the right competencies and other attributes required for the job, organizations can build a high-performance sales force capable of sustaining future growth.

Learning to apply the information you obtain during the hiring process to develop your newly hired employees will go a long way toward increasing the longevity of their tenure and reducing turnover.

THE HIGH COST OF SALES TURNOVER
How long does the average salesperson stay in a position? Top

1

salespeople will always be in demand, and their skills are easily portable from one sales environment to the next. Losing them to a higher bidder or a more lucrative sales opportunity is too easy to be taken lightly.

The cost of hiring a new employee for any position is significant regardless of whether an employee is fired or laid off or leaves voluntarily for a different company. There are many formulas that have been derived through research to calculate such costs. They vary widely but range upward of 200 percent of an employee's annual salary. That includes not only the obvious tangible costs of severance pay, vacation accrual, advertising, and relocation, but also the costs of routine hiring practices such as résumé review, recruiter fees, interview time, assessment, and then new-hire orientation and training.

Consider all the factors that contribute to calculating turnover costs. For each item, there are direct costs, for example, the recruiting agency or advertising fees, and indirect costs, such as the staff interviewing and administrative time. Some costs are even more unquantifiable; they might include customer dissatisfaction, poor employee morale, and loss of revenue during transitions.

Here are just some of the costs you should consider when estimating your cost of losing a sales employee:

◆ Exit administration for voluntary separation or firing
◆ Recruiting
◆ Interviewing
◆ Hiring
◆ Orientation
◆ Training
◆ Compensation and benefits while training
◆ Lost productivity
◆ Customer dissatisfaction
◆ Reduced or lost business
◆ Lost expertise
◆ Severance pay

Let's assume the average salary in a given company is $50,000 per year. If the cost of turnover is 150 percent of salary, then the cost of turnover in dollars would be $75,000 per employee leaving the company. For a mid sized company of 1,000 employees with a 10 percent annual rate of turnover, the annual cost of turnover is $7.5 million. What about a company with 10,000 employees? The cost of turnover is $75 million. Once you realize what it's costing, in both dollars and people assets, you'll want to take seriously how to reduce your turnover rate. So making the right hiring decisions and then supporting those decisions with targeted development is crucial to creating a high-performing sales team.

REDUCING YOUR TURNOVER

As you begin to look at ways to reduce your turnover, you should be able to answer all these questions:

- What is your annual turnover rate?
- What is your year-over-year average turnover rate?
- Can you tie significant changes in the rate to environmental factors?
- Are there times during the year when people leave with more frequency?
- What is your turnover rate compared to your competition?

Answering these questions will help you to understand all aspects of turnover within your sales force and provide insights in determining how to reduce turnover in your organization.

PITFALLS OF POOR HIRING DECISIONS

A Harvard University study reports that 80 percent of employee turnover can be attributed to mistakes made during the hiring process. The implications are huge: up to 80 percent of your turnover can be blamed on hiring mistakes. The problem lies in the employee selection process. Simply put, when you hire people for the wrong job, they leave.

Hiring the right people starts with understanding, describing, and correctly advertising the position you are hiring to fill. Starting with a definition of competency-based hiring, managers must learn how to define the soft skills and problem-solving skills required for the sales position, to assess, and to hire the best match.

Know Why Your People Leave

Be sure to conduct exit interviews and assess why your salespeople leave. While it can be difficult to get candid answers about personnel because often an employee who is leaving knows there is nothing to be gained (only lost) by saying anything negative, asking exiting employees to rate factors on a scale of 1 to 5 can point to the problems in a more objective and equally productive manner. You can ask them, for example, to rate the level of sales support, management support, fairness of sales goals, fairness of compensation, and so forth. Design your questions to determine whether you are creating an environment that salespeople can thrive in.

If you find those leaving feel that sales quotas are unattainable, or that they can't live on their compensation between sales, or that they simply think they can make more money someplace else, you'll have a better understanding of what you can do to change the environment.

INCREASE SALES FORCE RETENTION WITH BETTER HIRING PRACTICES

There are hiring practices you can implement that will help reduce your turnover and increase retention of your best people. Here are a few:

- ◆ Make attracting high performers part of your ongoing business practices.
- ◆ Define your hiring criteria so that you hire the right people for the job.
- ◆ Learn how to screen résumés for top performers.
- ◆ Give your hiring managers the skills they need to do the job right.

- Gather the right kind of data to ensure your candidates have the requisite skills.
- Create a consistent and thorough interview and selection process.
- Hire salespeople by looking at three areas: (1) experience, (2) technical skills, and (3) soft skills and problem-solving skills.

Hiring the right people starts with having a pool of quality candidates to choose from.

THE JOURNEY TO THE XC INSIGHT SYSTEM

I started my career in sales, and because I was successful, I eventually found myself working for a sales consulting firm, traveling the country offering companies sales training and sales talent management advice. What I found was that many of the companies I worked with didn't have the right talent matched to their positions and often didn't have the right sales leaders, either. So I suggested to the company I was working for that we could help our clients assess their talent, and these services would provide them value. Our company leadership didn't buy into the idea, feeling the company was profitable enough, and told me to continue doing what I was doing.

Eventually, I hired an executive coach who exposed me to my first personnel assessments. I started to research assessment companies both to determine what tools were available on the market to assess talent and also to figure out how the tools worked, because I was convinced these kinds of tools would be crucial for companies. Eventually, I started my own company and had the opportunity to put into practice what I had learned about assessments.

Initially, I distributed five assessment products that I felt were needed to get a complete enough view to determine whether a candidate was a good fit for a position. I knew that no single tool could do it, but using multiple assessments from multiple companies wasn't easy. Not only did I need to manage all five assessment systems and learn to administer and score them all, but I also had to get certified and licensed in all these areas. After about two years, even with all the certifications and tools, I was frustrated. No one system had all the components I wanted. Some had one component but not another, while others containing the missing components assessed some overlapping attributes with others. Managing the results was even more difficult and required me to completely customize and computerize a reporting system.

XC InSight System for Hiring and Developing Employees Is Born

It was then I decided I needed to develop my own system, one that incorporated all the pieces of the assessments I was using as well as a vision I had for other attributes, and most important, additional ways to use the data and make the data more practical to use. Thus began a six-year journey that started by learning all the requirements to develop a well-constructed test.

Based on more than 25 years of talent assessment experience, my company, XBInsight, was assessing multiple dimensions and providing some of the most sophisticated computerized reports available. Yet we knew there was so much more that could be done to coordinate data collection across multiple attributes and use the information collected in many more useful ways, such as:

◆ Provide more extensive assessments and results reports in a more efficient, user-friendly way, especially to make candidate comparisons easier

◆ Create more applications for the assessments and their results, not only to hire the right people, but also to provide an easier transition into their company, as well as give ongoing development support

◆ Update the research to ensure the measures reflect the modern workplace

Because I wanted to do it right, I hired nationally known scientists, industrial and organizational psychologists, and

PhDs to build and validate the XC InSight System. The assessment system we developed complies with all the U.S. government *Uniform Guidelines on Employee Selection Procedures* (a joint effort to provide guidance for the correct use of tests and other selection procedures in accordance with applicable rules developed by the Equal Employment Opportunity Commission and three other federal government agencies), the Society for Industrial/Organizational Psychology (SIOP) Principles, and the American Psychological Association (APA) Standards.

In addition to creating assessments held to the highest industry standards, the constant vision for development was translating data into meaningful, useful statements and visual graphics that anyone at any level could read, understand, and apply in real-world situations. We developed a new model for creating correlations among the data and applying the outcomes in new, more meaningful ways—an integrated system that displays the data from multiple aspects of the assessments, even multiple candidates, to present results in a highly readable and understandable format. The final result is the XC InSight System for hiring and developing employees.

Insights from XC InSight Development

Today, XBInsight, Inc. provides top-talent management services and over 50 products to make companies more profitable by optimizing employee selection, productivity, and development. XBInsight employs a trained team of expert coaches, trainers, and assessment analysts who use the XC InSight System to improve hiring practices and provide tools for developing and maintaining high-performance workforces.

The practices and advice in this book are based on the development and research for creating the XC InSight System and our international consulting experience in over 28 industries. We share the results of our validation, the specific attributes we recommend that you assess in hiring and development, and the best ways to combine assessments with other hiring and management practices. While these strategies are easier to implement with the XC InSight System, the information in this book should help you improve your assessment practices for any size business, whether you are looking at using assessments for the first time or want to review your current practices and find new ways to apply the assessment results in a more efficient and productive way.

HOW TO ASSESS FOR SOFT SKILLS AND PROBLEM-SOLVING SKILLS

There are many tools on the market that provide insights and information about candidates. Sometimes they provide surprising results, and other times they confirm with certainty what a candidate's track record shows. While the XC InSight System incorporates multiple assessment methodologies so that reporting coordinates and uses the results for greater efficiency, there are many assessment options on the market. Understanding their purposes and knowing what the assessments can measure will help any hiring manager make better choices and realize the many uses for the results. There are many types of assessments that measure a variety of attributes to ascertain the likelihood that a candidate will be a good fit.

A number of companies use more than one type of assessment because they view the information and the variety of perspectives as an investment in better hiring decisions. Looking at as many job-related attributes as possible—attributes tied to successful job performance—will increase the candidate-to-job match and help you make a more informed hiring decision. A comprehensive assessment system includes assessments of both a candidate's soft skills, such as communication preferences, interpersonal skills, and other attributes that characterize how a candidate will perform in a particular job environment, and the candidate's problem-solving skills, the cognitive skills and knowledge to successfully perform the job. Too often managers hire for the technical skills and fire for bad attitudes.

One of the chief advantages of using an assessment is having empirical and factual data—information that gives hiring managers something other than the candidate's word or a hiring manager's human interpretation when judging the top candidates. When you use well-constructed tests, candidates can't cheat or guess at the answers they think you want for a good job match. Unlike an interview situation, where it's easy to rely on your gut instincts, the assessment will confirm or contradict what you learn from the candidate interview.

Getting the right people into the right positions is only the first step. There are many other measures that contribute to employee longevity.

UNDERSTANDING AND DEVELOPING YOUR TALENT

Too often hiring managers glean valuable insights into employee preferences, strengths, and weaknesses during the hiring process and then fail to use the information as a resource to help develop and retain the employee. So rather than focusing exclusively on hiring, this book also simplifies developing sales employees by showing managers how to use the in-depth knowledge provided by assessments of sales employees. All that you learn during hiring can be used to continually improve the job–person fit.

THE SOLUTION

To hire the best, you need to use the best practices for making the perfect hire. This book presents the steps and information you need to determine how to hire, develop, and retain salespeople based on the research and best practices of the XC InSight System and the experience as a top-talent management company.

It's not enough today to have the right skills and abilities. Top employees also must demonstrate the right fit with organizational culture, mission, and values. In other words, top employees exemplify your brand. Identifying top performers leads to:

- Increased productivity

- Higher-quality work
- Reduced training time
- Higher retention
- Higher job satisfaction

All these factors contribute to higher profitability for companies. Hiring for the perfect fit along with developing your top performers creates a top-performing sales team.

MOVING FORWARD

Creating a hiring strategy will help you to develop a process to recruit top sales people and to avoid a revolving door of hiring and firing. Most hiring decisions are made based on technical skills and experience. Assessing your candidates' abilities to perform the job, with the addition of soft skills and problem-solving skills, will allow you to match the top candidates to your job requirements and to your organization. Once you get top sales talent, you need to figure out how to keep them happy. Part of establishing your strategy includes investing time and resources to develop and retain them. The next chapter discusses the first step in the solution to finding the perfect hire: creating performance standards or a clear definition for each job you need to fill.

Chapter

2 In the Beginning Step 1: Define the Job

The best and fastest way to learn a sport is to watch and imitate a champion.

—Jean-Claude Killy, Olympic Gold Medal Skier

HAVING A SYSTEMATIC, ONGOING PROCESS FOR HIRING WILL GIVE YOU A CLEARER path for hiring the right people for the job. Having a clearly defined job is the first step. Not only will it give you the best match between your candidates and the job that needs to be performed, it will also provide clear criteria to measure the performance of your new hire on the job. One theme you'll hear throughout this book is that you haven't completed the hiring process until your new hire is oriented, integrated into the job, and incorporated into a performance evaluation process that includes development. You need to have a clearly defined job before you can hire a new employee and subsequently create a plan to develop and evaluate performance.

Greenberg, Sweeney, and Weinstein state in their book, *How to Hire and Develop Your Next Top Performer*, that 20 percent of your workforce brings in 80 percent of the total revenue. Imagine how you could impact your bottom line if you were able to consistently hire more top performers. The goal of any hiring process is to identify the high-performer sales candidates. Normally, when we're hiring, what do we do? We evaluate the people to see if we can find the best person for a job opening. That is, we look at the metrics we think of for people in the position such as job experience, college degrees and majors, and so forth. In this chapter you learn to define the job so you can examine all aspects of the candidate attributes needed to successfully perform the job.

There are three areas of requirements to consider in your hiring process for finding top-performing salespeople: first, the technical skills required for the job; second, the necessary technical experience; and third, the soft skills and problem-solving skills needed. To adequately describe the job you are filling, you must provide the requirements for all these aspects.

> ### Don't Forget the Soft Skills and Problem-Solving Skills
>
> Too often we hire people for their technical skills, only to fire them because they can't problem-solve, develop rapport, or communicate effectively. Be sure your job definition addresses all aspects of the job requirements.

DEFINE THE JOB CRITERIA

First, you need to define the experience and the technical skills you are looking for to fill each position. To clearly define the job criteria, you have to create a concise description. A job description clearly and succinctly states the job requirements for the following areas: the responsibilities, activities, and tasks to be performed. The ultimate purpose is to provide as thorough an understanding of the job as possible. Too often job descriptions focus on the candidate requirements rather than explaining the responsibilities of the job.

Another common mistake is not rewriting a job description for each job you're hiring for. Let's say you're hiring for several sales positions at different levels. Instead of using one generic sales job description, write one for each level and variation. While many of the requirements you're seeking in a salesperson will be the same at each level, others will differ, so you need separate job descriptions that lay out those differences. These small differences can have a big impact on identifying the right candidates and the job satisfaction level of the subsequent new hire. Imagine thinking you will have broad responsibility for customer presentations only to find that in practice you only prepare the presentation for your supervisor.

The purpose of the description is twofold, both to explain the responsibilities and to attract the right level of candidates. As you move through the hiring process, you'll uncover additional information about the job that will help you refine and expand the job description. As important as it is to have a clear job description for hiring, the description is just as important for ongoing employee evaluation and development. Clearly identifying job responsibilities will provide areas for development and metrics for evaluating employee performance.

When companies are small, they often hire for very broad sales positions. As companies grow, the sales positions become more specialized. Without job descriptions, these specialized jobs become what an individual does to complete a job. In other words, the employees define their jobs based on what their experiences and capabilities are and what they see needs to be done. As companies move from small to mid sized, often there are many positions and levels, with a variety of titles, all defined by the people executing them or as the need arises for an incentive, pay raise, or some other external influence.

> **Dangers of Operating Without Job Descriptions**
> ◆ Difficult to identify consistent salaries and incentives
> ◆ No clear path for sales employee advancement
> ◆ No basis for determining sales performance criteria
> ◆ Difficult to determine who is performing at what level
> ◆ Difficult to identify training and development needs

Defining a job in sufficient detail will give you a stronger starting point for identifying high performers. Begin by identifying the job criteria. Here is a list of items to consider:

- **Job title and position.** Use industry-standard language for the job title and position whenever possible, for example, *entry-level sales support* or *district sales manager*. Be clear on the level of the job so you avoid attracting people who are overqualified or underqualified. A job title, scope of the territory, and level of responsibility all can help qualify the type of job you are filling.

- **Sales experience.** The number of years of experience will help people understand the level of the job and the salary level to expect. What kind of experience are you looking for? Does the candidate need a variety of experience to show growth or steadiness and satisfaction at a particular level?

- **Industry experience.** Does the job require industry-specific experience? For example, someone who has experience in the real estate industry will be more successful in another real estate company.

- **Technical skills.** Does the job require industry-specific knowledge or technical skills? Someone who is selling computer services will obviously need the technical skills to understand client needs.

- **Educational background.** Does the job require a minimum or maximum level of education? Are any special licenses or certifications needed? For example, an investment advisor has specific certifications and license requirements.

- **Availability.** Will the sales position require overtime, weekend or evening hours, or extensive travel? When a company assigns broad sales territories and offers products or services that call for demonstrations, inevitably that company will also require salespeople to travel.

- **Retention.** Clearly specify whether this is a short- or long-term position and whether there is opportunity for advancement. If you know this is a position to fill in for someone on leave, it's best to be up-front. Some employees are happiest as salespeople and will have no desire (or skill) for management; others will want to know if there is a path to a management position and will leave if they get on the job and find there isn't one.

Outline these aspects for every position in your organization and review the position each time you have a job opening to assure candidates fully understand the requirements of the job they are seeking and to attract the right candidates.

Using the job criteria, develop a job description that will help define the job further. Once you've drafted the job description based on the job criteria, then you'll want to take another look at the job requirements from the perspective of those who know the job.

INTERVIEW PEOPLE WHO KNOW THE JOB

Interview your top performers for their input on what it takes to perform the job. People who have performed a job will have the best insight to gather and document information on the specific behaviors, qualities, and characteristics important for success in the position. While this might not always be possible, especially if you are developing a new position within your company, when you have the opportunity to tap the knowledge of those who understand the job firsthand, it will help you identify high performer candidates more easily.

Your interview questions should be aimed very specifically at soliciting what differentiates the top performers in the job and what makes them successful. You can also interview managers to determine what they see as important for job success. To provide the kinds of information you need, you'll want to ask questions such as these:

- ◆ What are the typical tasks performed on a daily, weekly, or monthly basis?
- ◆ Are there additional responsibilities for which the job is accountable?

◆ What skill set and behaviors are required to support job success?

The results from these interviews will help you identify the broad tasks and activities for doing the job.

DEFINE THE SALES PERFORMANCE STANDARDS

Another helpful way to ensure clarity about the job is to show candidates how they will spend their time, what tasks and activities they will perform in any given week. This is in addition to the job description.

After developing a list of what it takes to perform the job based on the input from those in the position, you need to determine standards for performing each skill or activity. A performance standard is a concise statement that defines a specific and measurable outcome that the job must achieve for the organization to deliver superior performance. A performance standard must be measurable. Using this strategy will help you with development of the new hire because the employee shouldn't be held accountable for anything that doesn't have a definite measure.

To define a performance standard, decide how many hours per week each task or activity demands, and then evaluate the time required for each performance standard until the total reaches 80 percent of a normal workweek. So, for example, if you have a 40-hour workweek (although a high performer would never work only 40 hours), we take 80 percent, which is 32 hours. This leaves time for unexpected priorities driven from outside the job itself. Once you define the performance standards, prioritize them. That makes it clear what is most important for success in the job.

Let's look at a performance standard for the sales position of a New Business Development Account Manager (see Table 2-1). The No. 1 priority is new business development. It will require a salesperson to focus 10 hours a week on this activity. Then look at another performance standard: servicing an existing customer. That's 5 hours a week, and that priority is No. 2. The next priority is writing proposals. That's also probably going to take 5 hours a week. And continue until your total equals 32 hours.

Create a chart to define your performance standards for each position in your department or organization. It also helps new

Sales Representative Level 1, Performance Standards

Activity	Priority	Time Required
Making new business sales calls	1	10 hours per week
Servicing customers	2	5 hours per week
Writing proposals	3	5 hours per week
Returning phone calls and e-mails	4	7 hours per week
Doing paperwork	5	2 hours per week
Attending internal meetings	6	3 hours per week
Total hours for the week		32 hours

Table2-1. Defining Performance Standards

hires understand how they should allocate their time and efforts to be successful. When you've defined these standards for each job, you are better prepared to hire quickly, and you also have clear statements against which to compare candidates.

While this step may not appear essential, it will provide a concrete expectation for what a day in the life of a Level 1 sales position looks like and is another way to define the job.

MOVING FORWARD

Creating performance standards or a clear definition for the job is an important first step in your hiring strategy. Armed with the job criteria, a job description that includes the soft skills and problem-solving skills required for the job, and the performance standards, you are now ready to create step 2 in your hiring strategy called benchmarking the job. Benchmarking the job includes defining the job and provides you with the next step for making the right choice among your top sales candidates.

Chapter

3

Step 2: Benchmark the Job

Facts do not cease to exist because they are ignored.
—Aldous Huxley, British Writer

DEFINING THE JOB IS A CRITICAL STEP IN THE HIRING PROCESS, AND OFTEN THAT'S where companies stop. But using assessments that offer the capability for organizations to benchmark the job will help enormously in ensuring a match between candidates and the job. A customized benchmark for a job identifies the skills, abilities, and other characteristics to look for in potential candidates. Creating a benchmark is a process for ranking and identifying which skills, abilities, and characteristics are important for a salesperson to be successful in the job.

BENCHMARKING THE JOB

When you benchmark your sales position, you want to choose a validated assessment system that conforms to the EEOC Guidelines and is built on the most up-to-date research for measuring job-relevant skills and abilities for sales. Well-constructed assessment systems give you the opportunity for customization to ensure the assessment is clearly relevant to the job you are filling. Choose an assessment that includes a way for hiring managers, supervisors, human resources, or other subject-matter experts to match the specific job requirements with the skills the assessment measures.

Compare the Top and Bottom Performers

As part of the benchmark for your sales position, assess your current sales team) in the position and compare them to the benchmark. This will help to validate your benchmark. Do your current team's results match the skills and abilities that you are looking for in the job? The results also can provide you with a gap analysis of your current team. A gap analysis shows you if your salespeople in the job lack some of the requisite skills. That can help you identify the skills you'll need for your future hires.

JOB PROFILE OR BENCHMARK REPORT

The benchmark report in the XC InSight System is called the Job Profile Report. It identifies core competencies, core values, critical thinking skills, and work environment features that are important to a particular job based on the hiring managers' or subject-matter experts' input. The report is administered online and is used for comparing candidates with a particular sales job.

The XC InSight Job Profile process allows for the identification of core competencies and other characteristics and leads to a customized job profile. You can use the XC InSight Job Profile to:

- Provide descriptions of the key talents and experience a potential hire needs to possess to be successful in the job
- Create or update job descriptions
- Evaluate job candidates' potential for optimal productivity
- Create interview questions based on the competencies, core values, and critical thinking attributes relevant for the job

There are many assessment tools on the market, but not all allow for input to identify what a top performer needs for the job. In addition to creating a profile of the competencies, critical thinking skills, and core values for success on the job, a well-constructed assessment will also provide you with the questions you can ask to better identify the top candidates. Having system-generated questions will not only save you time, but also ensure your questions are job related and help determine your candidates' fit.

COMPETENCY INTERVIEW QUESTIONS

The following competency questions are examples based on competencies that may be required for a specific sales position:

Seizes Opportunities

- Give an example of a time when you needed to make substantial progress on a project while your supervisor was away. What did you do when you had questions or concerns about the project? What was the outcome?
- Describe a time when you undertook a project completely on your own initiative. What was the outcome?
- Cite an example of a time when you had to make a decision before all the facts had come in. What was the basis for your decision? What was the outcome?

Demonstrates Flexibility/Resilience

- Describe a time when you were criticized for your work. How did you respond to this?
- Detail a time when you had to perform your job in a rapidly changing work environment. How did you adapt?

Builds Customer Loyalty

- Describe a time when you connected with a customer who was hard to connect with at first. How did you get through to this customer?
- Provide a specific example of a time when you were recognized for providing excellent customer service. What did you do to gain this recognition?
- Give an example of a time when a customer asked you to do something that was unusual or out of the ordinary. How

did you respond to this customer? What was the outcome?

Gains Buy-In

- Describe a time when you helped two conflicting parties reach a compromise. How did you establish the terms of the compromise?
- Describe a time when you negotiated to make the terms of an agreement more favorable for your organization.

Establishes Credibility

- Describe a time when you had to alert someone to a mistake you made. What was your mistake? What prompted you to bring it to someone's attention? What was the outcome of your disclosure?
- Describe a time when someone challenged a decision you made. How did you respond? How, if at all, were you able to defend your decision?

You want to make sure that the assessment system you are using has the ability to customize these questions.

Core Value Questions

Knowing whether the candidate's core values are consistent with the hiring position will help ensure a better job fit. For example, if the candidate is looking for high-income potential and the position provides little or no incentive pay for high performance, there is a mismatch. If the person values personal relationships and is looking for a position with a great deal of human interaction but the job requires working independently in isolation, there is a mismatch. Here are sample questions for the top three core values for the benchmarked position of Sales Account Executive for New Business Development:

Achievement

- Describe a time when you had to push yourself in order to accomplish a difficult task at work. What were the circumstances? What steps did you take to accomplish your goal?
- Describe a time you had to motivate a coworker to successfully complete an assignment. What actions did you take?

- Provide an example of an on-the-job experience that you felt was particularly challenging. How did you respond? What was the outcome?

Social
- Describe your daily interpersonal interactions at work. Are they rewarding? Why or why not?
- Describe a time you helped a coworker who was struggling to finish a project on time. What led to your involvement? What steps did you take to assist him or her?

Power and Overt Influence
- Provide an example of a time when you emerged as the key leader for a project. What were your main objectives? How did you accomplish your objectives?
- Describe a project that allowed you to have more authority in the workplace. How comfortable were you with that authority?

Having many prepared questions for each competency and core value important for the job will enhance your screening and interviewing skills and create consistency if you are using multiple people for the process. Using interview questions that help you identify a person who fits in the sales role will go a long way to streamlining your hiring practices and improve your retention rate.

REFINE YOUR JOB DESCRIPTION

Once you've benchmarked the job, the Job Profile Report will provide a clear picture of what competencies, critical thinking skills, and core values are most important for the position—in other words, the soft skills and problem-solving skills required for top performance. With this additional information, you can revise the job description to more accurately reflect what's important to do the job and attract high performers.

Table 3-1 is an example of the kind of embellishment a Job Profile Report can provide to add more relevant information to your job description. This is what the Job Profile Report tells us for a Sales Account Executive for New Business Development. Especially in the skills section, you can see the competencies that were identified as important and most frequently used for the job are captured. The specific competency is in parentheses following the skill description.

Position/Title: Sales Account Executive for New Business Development

Purpose: The Sales Account Executive for New Business Development manages all aspects of the sales process to secure new customer contracts.

Responsibilities:
- Prospect and develop new relationships with local businesses.
- Write proposals and create presentations that offer customized marketing solutions for local businesses.
- Meet or exceed monthly/quarterly sales goals.
- Negotiate contract renewals.
- Sell multimedia solutions including print and online applications.

Specific Skills:
- Be proactive and take initiative/ownership for results. (Strive for Results)
- Handle multiple priorities in a fast-paced environment and diligently work toward goals. (Maintain Endurance)
- Anticipate and work through obstacles and accomplish tasks with minimal support or direction. (Seize Opportunities)
- Have effective communication skills, including showing enthusiasm, conveying information in an articulate, clear, and concise manner, and communicating with people from a variety of backgrounds (cultural, educational, etc.). (Communicate Articulately)
- Possess the ability to ask open-ended questions and summarize key points to build understanding. Engage others in dialogue and listen openly to others' opinions. (Listen Actively)
- Positively assert himself or herself and handle conflict and objections in a calm, effective manner. Present compelling rationale to support his or her position to influence and gain the commitment of others. (Persuade and Influence)

- Be able to adapt presentation style to the type of group. Maintain effective flow and pace when presenting, and convey information in a clear and concise manner. Use effective nonverbal communication when presenting, such as gestures, eye contact, or posture. (Deliver Compelling Presentations)
- Think constructively and draw conclusions when issues are vague. Understand complex written material, extract relevant information, and communicate to others in written form. (Reason Verbally)

Table 3-1. Job Description Additions from Job Profile Report

Having a Job Profile Report provides additional insights you can apply immediately, even before you begin the candidate selection.

MOVING FORWARD

Benchmarking the job provides you with a clear plan on the soft skills and problem solving skills required for the job. A benchmark will also provide you with interview questions that align with these skills. The results from benchmarking will not only provide a way to clarify the competency requirements for a job for a better sales candidate match, but will also provide more detailed descriptions you can add to the job description for attracting the right candidates, those who have the potential to be top performers. Before moving to step 3, interview and screen your top sales candidates, let's look in more detail at the kinds of attributes useful for benchmarking, and ultimately, candidate selection.

Chapter

4

Assessing the 3 Cs: Competency, Critical Thinking, and Core Values

Catch a man a fish, and you can sell it to him. Teach a man to fish, and you ruin a wonderful business opportunity.

—Karl Marx, German Political Theorist

WHEN YOU CHOOSE TO USE AN ASSESSMENT SYSTEM AS PART OF YOUR HIRING process, you'll want to measure multiple areas to get a complete picture of an individual's soft skills and problem-solving skills.

Even if you don't plan to use assessments, understanding the importance of knowing your candidates' qualifications in these areas will expand the kinds of questions you ask and consider in evaluating your candidates. In our research and experience, measuring competencies, cognitive abilities, and core values is important in identifying top sales talent.

MEASURING COMPETENCIES

There are some jobs where it's obvious that the primary criterion for job placement and success is competency. You want to be sure that an airplane pilot has the skills needed to take off, fly, and land a plane. Some qualifications can only be observed;

you want to be sure an NFL quarterback can throw the ball with precision. You will have greater assurance that someone is qualified for a position when you understand what competencies are required for the job and how an individual is to perform in the job. Understanding what kinds of competencies you can measure and how you can construct competency statements will help you create better job descriptions, more incisive candidate interview questions, and more relevant development plans.

When people think about candidate assessment, competency-based testing is usually what first comes to mind. It's the most commonly used tool to help identify and compare top job candidates. *Competence* is a broad term used for examining a person's level of fit within a role, the job of a salesperson, for example.

In some professions, hiring managers rely on licensing or certification exams to assess a person's competence. Doctors, lawyers, and other professionals have local, state, or national competency standards. Most of those assessments primarily measure the empirical content knowledge needed to perform the job.

For sales, you'll want to know that you've hired the right person for the specific sales job. An inside sales service position will differ from an external technical sales position and many other types of sales positions. You also want someone who has the required on-the-job experience, someone who can hit the ground running.

As a preview, this chapter

◆ Examines the history of competency as a way of measuring ability
◆ Defines job-specific competency statements
◆ Explores the difference between innate and tangible abilities
◆ Reviews task- and people-oriented competencies

Understanding the history of using competency to predict job performance will help put into context the importance of measuring multiple dimensions of a person's abilities, as well as the strengths and weaknesses to perform a specific job, for a better predictor of on-the-job success.

History of the Competency Model

To identify competency variables that predict job performance, McClelland compared individuals who clearly exhibited success on the job with those who were less successful in order to identify the characteristics or criteria associated with success. He also identified thoughts and behaviors related to successful outcomes by measuring competencies using open-ended questions where individuals responded to several well-defined alternatives to determine the behavior they would exhibit in a situation.

> ### The Modern Competency Movement
>
> David C. McClelland, PhD, Harvard professor and psychologist, known as the founder of the modern competency movement and best known for his research on workplace motivation and competence, promoted improvements in employee assessment methods. He advocated competency-based assessments and tests, arguing they were better than traditional IQ and personality-based tests. He documented his methods in his article "Testing for Competence Rather Than 'Intelligence'" (published in *American Psychologist* in 1973), which launched the competency movement in psychology.

Many large organizations called on McClelland to help with hiring practices following his groundbreaking article. When the U.S. Department of State asked him to improve its employee selection process, McClelland developed competencies for each position by:

- Studying the characteristics of the most effective officers and those considered average
- Conducting interviews to get detailed information about how individual officers handled the most critical situations they had experienced in their jobs

Gathering the knowledge, skills, and characteristics of those individuals who did a particular job well resulted in creating a standard for measuring success. This behavioral approach became the foundation for developing competency models, and McClelland's competency assessment method is the basis for the most reliable job competency models used today. Using this model identifies job-related competencies, so the assessment is a fair measure of whether someone has the skills to perform the job.

Components of a Clear Competency Statement

While there are many definitions, the competency models consistently identify two important elements for creating a clear competency statement:

- A competency comprises a knowledge and/or skills and is observable and measurable.
- The knowledge and skills distinguish superior performers from other performers.

Defining Competency

In 1995, several hundred human resource development experts at a conference in Johannesburg synthesized a comprehensive definition. Subsequently appearing in the article "The Quest for Competencies" by S. B. Parry, published in 1996 in *Training Magazine*, the definition is as follows:

A competency is a cluster of related knowledge, skills, and attitudes that affects a major part of one's job (a role or responsibility), that correlates with performance on the job, that can be measured against well-accepted standards, and that can be improved via training and development.

The behaviors that describe a competency combine four areas: abilities, personal characteristics, skills, and knowledge.

Based on McClelland's model, there are three stages for defining competencies:

1. Identify the foundation of *inherent talents* (*aptitude* and *personal characteristics*).
2. Identify the *acquired learning* or *tangible abilities* (*skills*

and *knowledge*) that are gained through learning, effort, and experience.

3. Then combine the aptitude and personal characteristics, the skills and knowledge, so they work together as a specific set of *behaviors* that describe a job-related competency.

The competency pyramid in Figure 4-1, based on McClelland's model, displays the formation of a competency.

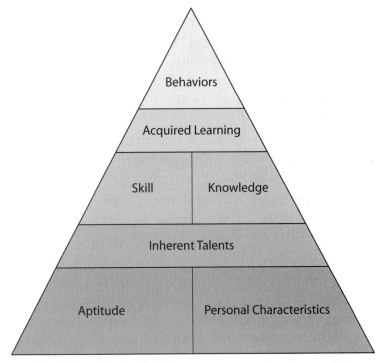

Figure 4-1. Competency pyramid

The following explanations of each stage in the model show in greater detail how the pyramid builds into a competency.

Inherent Talents

Aptitude and personal characteristics combine to identify the inherent talents required for a specific sales competency.

Aptitude is defined as an innate talent that suggests a potential to acquire or use a particular type of skill or knowledge. Have you ever referred to another's abilities by saying something such as, "John really has a knack for numbers." When you make that kind of statement, you are more likely referring to John's aptitude or innate talent for mathematics.

A person with a mathematical aptitude usually demonstrates a potential for acquiring accounting skills. Other examples of aptitudes can include mechanical ability or an affinity for detail work. In sales the most likely aptitudes will be comfort in communicating, building rapport, and developing relationships with people. A natural inclination for problem solving is another important aptitude for today's salesperson. Closing a sale is no longer a matter of demonstrating a product; it requires translating how a product or service solves a prospect's problem.

Since aptitudes are innate: A person comfortable communicating with people will be able to master presentation skills more quickly.

That being said, even traits that are innate can be modified and developed; however, the learner without innate talent will need more training and require more effort.

Personal characteristics, which are also innate, include personality traits that demonstrate a way of relating to the environment such as self-confidence or emotional stability. These can indicate a disposition for dealing with certain types of situations, roles, or functions. For example, someone who has self-confidence is more likely to succeed when cold-calling prospects.

Acquired Learning

The next stage in developing a competency looks at the acquired learning, the skills and knowledge that people learn and acquire from experience and training.

A developed *skill* can be referred to as an expertise. Skills can reflect:

◆ Tangible abilities such as the ability to write a sentence that clearly presents an idea

- Less tangible capabilities, such as the ability to think strategically or persuade others

Knowledge is acquired through learning and experience and can be:

- Tangible and easily measured, for example, having adequate knowledge of a particular product
- More complex, for example, having knowledge of the workings of a particular financial market and the effects on global developments

Combined, these are the tangible abilities reflecting what a person has learned or acquired.

Behaviors

Combining the acquired learning and inherent talents yields a behavior that is demonstrated in a salesperson's job.

Behaviors depict the multidimensional abilities that define a competency that is being demonstrated in a job.

Behaviors can be modified and taught. For example, while it might be difficult for a person lacking empathy to develop a trait related to empathy, through training and development that person can learn to use empathetic behaviors such as listening to the needs of others and addressing concerns.

Forming a Competency

A well-developed competency statement is one that successful salespeople demonstrate on the job and includes all the competency building blocks. Here's an example of building a competency statement that shows how all the factors contribute to one of the top required sales job competencies:

Develops and Maintains Relationships

- John is naturally very confident and comfortable relating to others. Even as a child, people noted that he was a "people person." (Personal characteristics)
- John's degree in the field of communications, various training, and on-the-job experience have helped him to become a very skilled presenter. (Skills and knowledge)

◆ John conveys information in an articulate, clear, and concise manner and communicates well with people from a variety of backgrounds (cultural, educational, and so forth). John is able to assert himself and handle conflict and objections in a calm, effective manner. He presents compelling rationale to support his position in order to influence and gain the commitment of others. John uses effective nonverbal communication when presenting, such as gestures, eye contact, and posture. (Behaviors)

The competency statement, to be used for evaluating and developing John's job skills, identifies the dominant personal characteristics, skills and knowledge, and behaviors required for one of the important competencies for all sales positions, Develop and Maintain Relationships.

Understanding competency statements should provide a clearer picture of why assessing for competencies related to the job can provide valuable information for selecting and developing top sales talent.

Sample Validated Sales Competencies

The competencies shown in Table 4-1 have been validated (shown to be used on the job) based on extensive research for the XC InSight System. These are the competencies you will want to benchmark against each job you are seeking to fill, to identify which are the most relevant and most important. These are competencies described at the broadest level.

Task-Oriented Competencies
◆ Delivers Compelling Presentations
◆ Demonstrates Curiosity
◆ Enjoys Winning
◆ Maintains Endurance
◆ Manages Work
◆ Recognizes Growth Opportunities
◆ Strives for Results

Table 4-1. Validated Sales Competencies for Success on the Job in Sales

- Strives for Success

People-Oriented Competencies
- Builds Customer Loyalty
- Builds Collaboration
- Communicates Articulately
- Demonstrates Flexibility/Resilience
- Develops and Maintains Relationships
- Displays Emotions Effectively
- Displays Fairness and Objectivity
- Establishes Credibility
- Exudes Confidence
- Gains Buy-In
- Listens Actively
- Persuades and Influences

Table 4-1. Validated Sales Competencies for Success on the Job in Sales (continued)

Behaviors Associated with Each Competency

You may have noticed that the list in Table 4-1 classifies competencies as task oriented or people oriented. *Task-oriented* competencies are self-descriptive and refer to undertakings that involve accomplishing a job or assignment. *People-oriented* competencies require effectiveness in work areas that primarily involve interpersonal interactions. All competencies can be classified in one category or the other. As you can see in the list of validated sales job competencies, the majority are people oriented. The people-oriented competencies tend to be more important and used more frequently than the task-oriented ones. So when you benchmark your specific job, you might expect the people-oriented competencies to be well represented in the final sales job profile. Still, all sales jobs are different, so that might not always be the case.

Once you've defined the competencies that are required for superior performance for your sales position, you need to examine the behaviors that are associated with each. These should be formed for you within the competency that you've chosen as part of the assessment system you are using. Table 4-2 presents an example of the behaviors associated with the competency Develops and Maintains Relationships.

Develops and Maintains Relationships
- Works to build and maintain friendly, warm relationships
- Regularly keeps up with contacts
- Genuinely shows personal interest in others
- Builds long-term, solid relationships
- Is approachable
- Keeps conflict from being personal
- Maintains open and regular lines of communication with customers and coworkers
- Builds effective working relationships with other departments and functions
- Establishes effective working relationships outside the organization
- Leverages informal networks to get things done

Table 4-2. Example of Behaviors Associated with a Competency

It's more often a lack of the soft skills that lead to firing someone. Similarly, we fail to help employees develop their soft skills. By listing the task- and people-oriented skills separately, you can see which have the greatest weight for a particular job. Is this job one that is people oriented or task oriented? When you choose an assessment, look to see whether it includes both people- and task-oriented competencies. The XC InSight System has a customized feature to define these for each sales competency that you determine is most important to your sales position.

As important as identifying the competencies that contribute to success in the sales position is the assessment construction itself. Many candidates now train for interviews and interview assessments, so they can manipulate their answers by anticipating the job requirements and the optimal answers to the questions. Our latest research suggests that competency assessments that are based on past performance (or biodata, which are biographically based facts such as work history) make it more difficult for candidates to lie about what they've done and how they've performed in the past. Another reason this method of assessment is so popular is the way it identifies an employee's strengths and weaknesses in comparison with the job requirements.

Questions that don't relate specifically to the job, are not used in the hiring decision, or don't contribute to strengthening an employee's skills are a waste of time.

For entry-level positions, be aware that someone may not have had a chance to demonstrate a particular competency in past positions, yet the candidate might be capable of performing it given the chance. That's why it's important that the assessment you choose measures multiple areas. For example, you may see in a candidate's cognitive results that the person has the ability, but the competency results may show that he or she has not mastered the skill. This is important to consider when assessing entry-level candidates to fill your positions.

Competency assessments that are validated for selection and develop-

> ### Why Use Competency Assessments?
>
> Competency assessments can provide a valuable tool for employee development, coaching, and training. Some of the benefits of evaluating competencies for your sales team include:
>
> ◆ Aligning individual goals with company goals
> ◆ Providing individuals with focus on those areas that have the greatest impact on their overall effectiveness and performance
> ◆ Aligning development opportunities with the organization's requirements for success
> ◆ Providing a framework for ongoing coaching

ment will provide initial support in the hiring process but have added value when the information can be used immediately for creating a development plan and ongoing employee–manager support tools. Another measure to help you in hiring decisions is assessing candidates' cognitive ability.

MEASURING COGNITIVE ABILITIES

Over the years there has been much debate on the topic of intelligence versus competence and how they relate to job performance. In lay terms, intelligence, also called cognitive ability, measures how smart someone is. IQ tests measure people's general knowledge, relative to their age. They measure what a person knows more from an academic setting rather than life skills and experience.

Taking an adult IQ test, you might find multiple-choice questions such as "What is the capital of Italy?" or "Who wrote the novel *A Connecticut Yankee in King Arthur's Court?*" Or you might be confronted with a mathematical word problem that requires knowledge of algebra to solve. The majority of intelligence testing does not relate to any specific work role, but rather says, all else being equal, people who are smarter have a greater likelihood of excelling in a job. Decades of research show that there is value in measuring both competence and intelligence.

So being able to identify strengths and weaknesses for an individual's cognitive ability in relation to what's most important for a sales position will help in hiring the right candidate. In conducting research for the cognitive ability component of the XC InSight System, we identified critical thinking skills, because a person's critical thinking ability reflects aptitude or a general level of intelligence.

History of Measuring Cognitive Abilities

Modern psychological theory views cognitive ability as multidimensional. On a general level, cognitive ability (IQ) tests measure the ability to:

◆ Solve problems
◆ Learn a specific job
◆ Understand instructions
◆ Apply knowledge to new situations
◆ Benefit from job training

- Communicate clearly
- Reason logically
- Comprehend relationships in a business setting

A century of scientific research shows that general cognitive ability predicts a broad range of important life outcomes, behaviors, and performances, including academic achievement, job performance, and creativity. Cognitive ability is at the core of psychology and affects all aspects of our lives.

What is most important about the research is that general cognitive ability predicts job performance across jobs without bias toward any particular field, industry, or job level.

Defining Cognitive Abilities

The XC InSight System's cognitive assessment is called critical thinking.

Purposes for Assessing Cognitive Ability

Assessment results can provide insight into the strengths and weaknesses of a candidate's cognitive ability. There are two primary purposes that the Critical Thinking (cognitive) Profile can serve:

Candidate selection. Assessing critical thinking can assist a hiring manager in the selection process by assessing a candidate's cognitive ability or ability to reason through and analyze complex problems or data. The manager can compare the candidate's scores with those of others and determine if a candidate's abilities are aligned with those of the benchmarked job.

Succession planning. Similar to the application for candidate selection, the critical thinking data for an employee can be compared with a benchmarked job to determine if the employee's abilities are aligned with those of that specific job and also to identify gaps.

Critical thinking is defined as the ability to reason through and analyze complex problems or data, use insight to generate novel ideas and solutions, and effectively integrate abstract thinking with practical intelligence. The XC InSight System identifies three facets of critical thinking necessary for on-the-job performance:

- **Reasons Logically.** Able to deal with multiple issues and demands. Uses logic and reasoning to identify the strengths and weaknesses of alternative solutions, conclusions, or approaches to problems. Reviews related information to develop and evaluate options and implement solutions. Demonstrates mental alertness to spot relationships and opportunities for improvement.
- **Reasons Numerically.** Ability to analyze data, draw conclusions, and reason based on numbers. Demonstrates comfort with quantitative data.
- **Reasons Verbally.** Demonstrates an ability to think constructively, identify themes, and think on an abstract level. Understands concepts framed in words.

Once hiring managers complete a job profile to benchmark the job, they are able to define relevant behaviors within each of these areas that are important to superior performance. For a job requiring the ability to reason logically, for example, someone who can respond easily to objections and questions as part of the sales process should score comparatively well in the critical thinking area of Reasons Logically. Table 4-3 offers an example of the more detailed, relevant behaviors for the critical thinking skill Reasons Logically.

Reasons Logically
- Gathers data from a variety of sources to make decisions
- Determines whether action is required when issues or problems are identified
- Develops and evaluates alternative options to address issues or problems
- Probes below the surface to identify underlying causes of issues or problems
- Identifies strengths, weaknesses, opportunities, and threats of alternative options, scenarios, or business activities
- Recognizes the validity of multiple approaches to solving problems
- Critically reviews, analyzes, and interprets information

Table 4-3. Specific Job Success Skills for Reasons Logically

- ◆ Draws conclusions from incomplete information
- ◆ Has high attention to relevant detail
- ◆ Keeps a long-term perspective
- ◆ Is tolerant of ambiguity
- ◆ Recognizes patterns, trends, and relationships
- ◆ Quickly understands and orients to new information
- ◆ Manages multiple or competing issues and demands
- ◆ Identifies and fills in gaps in information
- ◆ Integrates data to identify trends, problems, and issues

Table 4-3. Specific Job Success Skills for Reasons Logically (continued)

To ensure a good hire, it's critical to have clear competencies and know which are most important for the job. Another area often overlooked is values.

MEASURING VALUES

Understanding one's core values provides insights into the type of work and work environment most motivating or appealing, rewarding, and important. Individuals who work with people and in environments that best fit their values are more satisfied and perform at a higher level. An individual's values reflect a person's underlying beliefs and priorities about what he or she finds rewarding. When we have a clear understanding of others' core values, we can communicate more effectively with them.

Knowing what motivates individuals and comparing their chief motivators can provide many insights of which managers and individuals might not otherwise be aware.

Here are some examples showing how sales managers can apply their understanding of values and what motivates individuals in the workplace.

Hiring

As one part of an assessment for hiring, values can help you understand how well a candidate will fit with the benchmarked job. When candidates' core values and motivators align with the position, they will more likely be happy in the job. Core values alignment alone will not predict success; it indicates what kind of work candidates prefer, not whether they are qualified to perform in the job.

Development

Core values are the underlying forces that drive behavior. Understanding how core values impact success is a key ingredient of self-awareness and development. People are more likely to thrive in a role that rewards those things they are most passionate about. For example, individuals who are passionate about self-enhancement and who set and work toward achieving challenging personal goals will likely be energized in a professional role that measures success based on attainment of goals.

When individuals are aware of what motivates them, then they will have better insights for a rewarding career path. Being aware of what motivates them along with the other components of an assessment, they can start to understand what skills and other areas they need to develop to achieve their goals.

Despite being relatively stable, core values can, and do, shift over time and as individuals move through adulthood. The importance placed on a specific value can grow or diminish. For instance, an individual who highly valued adventure early in his or her career may value this less over time with age and lifestyle changes and begin to emphasize other values, such as power. Many organizations use socialization and training programs for new employees, attempting to further communicate, strengthen, and develop the organization's values within their employees.

HISTORY OF THE VALUES MODEL

Our beliefs, values, and attitudes take shape early in life. Depending on the adults or figures of influence in children's lives, children will learn, mirror, or imitate those actions as they become adolescents and adults. We learn that we can choose to change those beliefs, values, and attitudes as we gain new knowledge and have new experiences, but researchers think that our attitudes and values develop through stages in our relationship to stimuli such as conflict, stress, or even pain. They can also develop through experiencing pleasure, satisfaction, and joy. Every day we are faced with real situations that call for thought, decision, opinion, and action. Consciously or subconsciously, every decision, reaction, or course of action arises from our beliefs, our values, and our attitudes; and a better understanding of how beliefs are formed, what values are, and how attitudes are shaped helps us communicate more effectively. Many theorists and researchers have studied the basic concepts of values and how they are formed. Two of the most influential individuals are Eduard Spranger and Shalom H. Schwartz.

Spranger on Values

Eduard Spranger, a German psychologist and teacher, wrote in his book, *Types of Men: The Psychology and Ethics of Personality*, that people are driven to act on their values based on experiences and beliefs.

He concluded that:

◆ There are six attitudes or world views: theoretical, utilitarian, aesthetic, social, individualistic, and traditional.
◆ People discover and understand the world differently.
◆ By understanding someone's personal interests, attitudes, and values, we realize why they behave a certain way.

Spranger discovered that certain values drive us into action, and the stronger our values, the more passionately we will pursue something. He states that our top two attitudes dictate what we value positively. The second two values may, depending on the situation, be important to us; whereas the last two values are not likely to drive our behaviors much at all.

Values help us understand why people behave a certain way. Values help to answer the question, "What is important in our lives?"

- Security
- Independence
- Wisdom and knowledge
- Success and achievement
- Kindness
- Pleasure

Since the 1950s, a general consensus has emerged regarding the most useful way to conceptualize basic values.

Schwartz on Values

Shalom H. Schwartz in his work, *Basic Human Values*, defines the concept of values in the following way:

- Values are beliefs. These beliefs are tied to emotion and not necessarily objective ideas.
- Values are motivational by nature and refer to the desirable goals people strive to attain.
- Values guide the selection of actions for a particular situation.
- Values are ordered by importance relative to one another. An individual's values form an ordered system of value priorities that tend to characterize an individual.

Schwartz says that values are desirable goals that go across situations, that vary in importance, and that serve as guiding principles in people's lives. The distinguishing factor among values, according to Schwartz, is the type of motivational goal or factor represented. While other inventories had been developed to measure values, the Schwartz Values Survey was the first instrument developed to measure values and motivators.

The XC InSight System is based on the research and writing of both Spranger and Schwartz, yet incorporates language and assessment techniques that focus more specifically on the work environment than the general population.

With an awareness of your sales team's value system and how it shapes overall behavior, you can develop new strategies to increase their success. Just imagine if you could simply change the words you are using and cause a tremendous, productive reaction from your sellers, and better yet, your buyers. Words are powerful, but unless you know what factors motivate each person, your chances of choosing the correct words are slim.

Looking at the history of the values model and how we've come to realize the importance of values provides a more complete framework for understanding the role that values and motivation play in the lives of salespeople and their work environment.

What Workplace Values Can Tell Us

Looking at values results or profiles from an assessment designed for the work environment, you will glean the following insights:

♦ An individual's values reflect his or her underlying beliefs and priorities about what he or she finds rewarding.

♦ Understanding one's values provides insights into the type of work and work environment that might be motivating or appealing.

♦ Individuals who work with people and environments that best fit their values are more satisfied.

♦ The top three values are typically the ones that will drive an individual's actions and decisions.

Using best practices in doing our research, we identified eight values that reflect today's work environment. Table 4-4 on the next page divides the values into three categories and defines each value. Note that most values assessments on the market today are based on values that relate to the general population rather than the workplace.

Conceptual, Creativity, and Adventure values provide insight into how an individual prefers to engage at work. These tell us about one's openness to change and preferences for stability and provide insights into the types of tasks that one finds stimulating.

The values of Independence, Achievement, and Power and Overt Influence, on the other hand, provide information about an individual's self-enhancement and self-reliance motives and the emphasis an individual places on developing and asserting himself or herself.

Core Value: Stimulation

Identifies how people approach their work and the type of work that is most stimulating.

Conceptual. Those who score high in Conceptual prefer work that is mentally stimulating and requires a high level of mental ability. They like to be seen as an expert, enjoy solving complex problems, and seek out learning opportunities to keep an active mind.

Creativity. Those who score high in Creativity enjoy opportunities to be imaginative and inventive. They like to develop new ideas, methods, and interpretations and are driven by the need to express themselves in an original way.

Adventure. Those who score high in Adventure are comfortable with unpredictability, thrive on taking calculated risks, and work well under pressure. They enjoy novel situations, like competition, and tend to be thrill seekers.

Core Value: Individualism

Provides information on an individual's self-enhancement and self-reliance motives. It focuses on the emphasis that individuals place on developing and asserting themselves.

Achievement. Those who score high in Achievement are driven to accomplish challenging goals. They push for results, stretching themselves and others to achieve more.

Power and Overt Influence. Those who score high in Power and Overt Influence seek recognition, prestige, authority, and control. They want to be respected by others and be seen as successful. Influencing others is a source of satisfaction, and these individuals enjoy roles that require them to make decisions that are imple-mented by others.

Independence. Those who score high in Independence desire autonomy and prefer having flexibility and freedom in their job. These individuals take the initiative and set their own course based on their own judgment. Following the rules has lower priority.

Table 4-4. Values defined

Table 4-4. Values defined (continued)

Altruism and Social core values provide insight into an individual's motives to connect and relate to others. These help us understand the importance that an individual places on having contact with or helping others.

Understanding core values provides insight into what drives behavior and what type of work and work environment are most motivating to each individual. When using values assessment for selection, it's useful to look at the values profile of your existing team, as well. Candidates who align with the benchmarked job as well as the other team members will be a better fit. The results will also show areas of development for your current team.

MOVING FORWARD

There are many types of hiring assessment tools on the market today that can provide data on your candidates. Understanding how to choose among them and learning about the attributes hiring assessments should measure are an important ingredient in hiring strategy. The three areas you can test for that will help you choose the best among your top sales candidates include competencies, cognitive ability, and core values.

Knowing about what we can measure for benchmarking and the value of the information these dimensions can provide you with a solid process for starting your candidate search, the third step in your hiring strategy.

Chapter

5

Step 3: Screen and Interview

Do not demand accomplishment of those who have no talent. Do not charge people to do what they cannot do. Select them and give them responsibilities commensurate with their abilities.
                              —Sun Tzu, Great Chinese Military Thinker

HAVING A SYSTEMATIC, ONGOING PROCESS FOR HIRING WILL GIVE YOU A CLEARER path for hiring the right people for your sales position. It will also help you to be a hiring-ready company, one that can respond immediately, whether it's to fill an unexpected vacancy, expand to meet increased customer demand, or fill gaps in your current employee needs.

HIRING READY

Most managers wait until they have an opening to begin recruiting salespeople. This is often a recipe for unnecessary confusion and places urgent demands on everyone involved in the hiring process. Remember the saying "You are only as good as your people." Attracting top-notch talent is essential to your sales success and should be an ongoing part of your business operations. Rather than wait until you have an opening, build your network of candidates and a program for consistently searching for them. Follow their progress and serve as a mentor during their career development.

Here are some of the ways you can incorporate good hiring practices as part of your search for high-performing salespeople.

Review Unsolicited Résumés

Instead of filing or discarding unsolicited résumés, review them as they come and then be proactive. If you get résumés that look good, talk with the applicants even if you don't have any openings at the time. It gives you an opportunity to identify potential candidates for future openings and, at the same time, impress high-quality candidates with your company's offerings. When there is an appropriate opening, you might find that even though your candidate is already in another position, because of the connection you've made, he or she is willing to consider the opportunity.

Use Multiple Recruiting Sources

Few companies are fortunate enough to find the right candidate on the first try. Instead, the likelihood of finding the best candidate increases in relation to the size of the talent pool. You need to use multiple recruiting sources to help maximize your talent pool. Many employers and hiring managers use only one or two sources for identifying employees. There are many options that can increase the numbers. Here are some:

- ◆ Colleges, universities, and other educational certification and licensing agencies with job placement offices. Often underestimated, these organizations are not only for hiring entry-level people. Many schools offer their alumni ongoing placement services.
- ◆ Public and private employment agencies. Develop relationships with placement personnel within these organizations to provide screening consistent with the job description and hiring criteria.

- ◆ Professional recruiters. Keep a list of recruiters with a track record of top-performing candidates.

Build Your Network

Keep a simple top 20 list. Write the names of 20 people that you can e-mail who have contact with many of the kinds of people you are looking to hire. Then, when you are ready to hire, put together a two-paragraph e-mail describing your company and the kind of person you want to hire, along with the job description. Make it a point to call the people on your list as quickly as possible and let them know you are e-mailing the summary. Follow up a week later to see if they know anyone who fits your description or if they at least know someone who might know someone.

Reward Employee Referrals

Recognize or reward your employees for identifying job candidates. Often your best source for new employees comes from those within. Happy, productive employees will want to surround themselves with people they trust to do a good job, who will add value to the company. They often have experience working with others in previous jobs.

Be the Company Everyone Wants to Work For

Increase your organization's visibility as a top employer. People form impressions about a company based, in part, on their interactions with the organization's products, advertising, employees, and community involvement. These are excellent ways to demonstrate your organization's values and culture to potential employees.

Make sure that when posting a sales job opening, you paint the best possible picture. Keep it realistic and accurate (don't overpromise and underdeliver), but be sure that you highlight the best of what your company has to offer. Are there statistics, awards, or differentiating advantages you can boast about? Whether it's a best product award you've won, a below-industry-average turnover rate the company has, or a shared job program you offer, you can increase your company's attractiveness to candidates.

Be Easy to Find

Make sure that your sales positions are always posted on your website. Use common terminology so candidates searching the Internet will be able to find your position easily.

There are a few basics to hiring that can go a long way to making sure you're getting the right people. The companies that get the best applicants tend to get a lot of people applying for each position. The general quality of the pool is high, such that if you had to decide by throwing darts at a list of potential employees, you likely would make a great decision. So ask yourself the question, "Did we get a lot of high-quality people to apply for the position?"

Generally speaking, you should have an initial pool of 50 high-quality applicants from which to choose. If you are relying on your network of contacts to find someone, are you reasonably sure they have a large enough pool of high-quality people whom they can access? Remember, high performers tend to surround themselves with high performers, so only go to your high-performer network of friends. This is why a company that has established a stellar reputation in its industry is able to continue to hire stellar people.

By being a hiring-ready company on the lookout for high-performing salespeople, you'll build a reservoir of contacts when you need to hire.

To make the right selection decisions takes a commitment to understand both the position and the candidates from many perspectives and dimensions. Once you've done some initial work, repeat hiring will happen more easily, in a less urgent manner, with more consistent results. You'll also learn how to help new hires adapt more quickly, and to develop and retain them.

SCREEN FOR CONSIDERATION

If you've been doing a good job of creating a wide pool of candidates to consider, you'll want to pare down your search to the top candidates. Here are some ways you can further refine your candidate pool to be sure final consideration is given to high performers.

Review Résumés

Wouldn't your life be easy if the right résumés leaped to the top of the heap, the way those high performers themselves do once you've hired them? It's possible to spot the high performers who can help your organization excel—just by reading their résumés. A well-written résumé provides many clues for hiring managers to single out the best candidates. Here are some of the accomplishments you should look for in sales candidates:

- How their contribution and sales expertise benefited previous companies
- Specific sales figures (dollar or percentage increase)
- How well they met their quota or other sales expectations
- Awards or honors earned
- Salvaging of accounts that were previously languishing
- Innovation or role in product development or a new-product launch
- Sales training programs attended or delivered to continually improve performance
- How their part in contract negotiations resulted in a positive business deal
- Committees or boards they served on or special projects they participated in
- Their work with nonprofit organizations to raise money to lead or grow a cause
- Involvement in competitive activities such as sports
- Track record of success in job (how quickly it took them to become successful)
- Use of computer skills or technology to maximize efficiency

Here is a detailed list of what else you should look for when screening candidates' résumés. Stan-dard résumés include information regarding an individual's educational background, employment experience, and technical skills.

Educational Background

♦ College and graduate school
♦ Professional certifications
♦ Professional sales training

Sales Experience

♦ Previous sales support experience
♦ Previous sales experience
♦ Outside sales experience
♦ Commission-based sales
♦ Major or national account sales

Industry Experience

♦ Direct competitive sales experience
♦ Knowledge of customer base
♦ Existing customer relationships
♦ Knowledge of territory

Knowledge and Technical Skills

♦ General product knowledge
♦ Technical skills
♦ Organizational skills
♦ Office skills
♦ Computer skills

> ### Resume Review Tip: High-Performing Salespeople Change Jobs Often
>
> Don't be surprised, dismayed, or deterred by the number of jobs or positions that a high performer has had. It's no longer the norm for people to stay in one job for many years. And because of their drive to succeed, high performers in sales are always looking for new opportunities to move up. An employer who cannot offer those opportunities won't hang onto them for long. If you can offer advancement and challenge to high performers and if their résumés show a constant progression upward in terms of position and responsibilities, a candidate who has switched employers a lot is probably worth interviewing.

Communication and Presentation Skills
- Communication skills
- Writing ability
- Telemarketing skills
- Cold-calling skills
- Foreign languages skills

There is much a résumé can tell you before setting up costly interviews to identify employees with high potential for success. With a clearly defined job description and résumés screened for hiring the high performer, you are ready to begin telephone screening and interviewing.

TELEPHONE SCREENING

Before scheduling face-to-face time with all the candidates under consideration, conduct telephone interviews and refine your final list. It's important to have an efficient and effective method for conducting phone interviews. Create your phone screening questions using the specific and most important job criteria you've identified. When you use an assessment that provides the questions based on the competencies and core values most important for the job, this step will be more consistent, productive, and relevant for matching a job and candidate. Telephone screening will help you determine if a candidate has what it takes to move to the next level in your interviewing process and can save you from spending valuable time interviewing candidates who would not be a good fit. You can reduce the time spent in the overall process and spare the inconvenience of travel for those who do not qualify.

Once you've narrowed your candidates to those you feel are the best match to your position, then you're ready for the face-to-face interview.

INTERVIEWING CANDIDATES

The interview process is an opportunity to develop a personal relationship with the candidates to determine how they interact and communicate. If multiple interviewers are involved, it's helpful to follow these guidelines to ensure thoroughness, consistency across candidates, and objectivity during the process. Here's the outline of a process that will ensure consistency in your interviewing process:

- So that interviewers prepare in advance of the meeting, provide each one a folder with the specific job description, performance standards you developed, and the candidate's resume.
- Provide the interviewers with the related competency, behavioral, and core values questions based on the job profile. If many people are involved in conducting the interviews, you can give each person different aspects of the job to focus on with the candidate, as long as you have sufficient overlap with multiple views on each aspect so there is more than one person's perspective.
- Create a comfortable environment for your candidate. Be on time. Start by spending a few minutes chatting informally to put the candidate at ease. Meet where you will avoid any interruptions.
- Take notes during the interview and review immediately following. Make sure you can evaluate the candidate based on facts rather than recall, which can become unclear as time passes. It's too easy to confuse one candidate's interview responses with another's when time passes before you make the hiring decision.
- Create an interviewer evaluation form to compile all interviewer responses. Immediately following the session, have each interviewer evaluate the candidate on the areas he or she was assigned.
- Compare the interviewer responses. Where there are discrepancies, ask the two interviewers to review their experiences with each other and come to a consensus.

[This list is based in part on editors Susan H. Geblein et al.,

Successful Manager's Handbook, 7th ed. (ePredix, Inc.: Minneapolis, 2004, p. 201).]

Once you've screened and interviewed those you consider your top candidates, compare them against the benchmark that you've established. The primary purpose of the interview, however, will be to identify the top candidates, unless you choose not to invest in assessments. Interview questions can only go so far, especially since some job seekers have made a career out of preparing for

---

Effective Interview Tips

◆ Set a goal of having the applicant do 80 percent of the talking.

◆ Learn to differentiate good information from sizzle. Good information usually contains specific behaviors that the candidate has engaged in, while sizzle information sounds good but means little and serves to falsely inflate your evaluation of a candidate.

◆ Be comfortable with silence after you have asked a question. This will allow the candidate time to think and take initiative.

◆ Display energy and show enthusiasm for the job for which you are interviewing candidates.

◆ Prepare for the interview by reviewing the candidates' résumés and practicing the specific questions you plan to ask.

---

interviews, masking their responses to conform to what they know the job requires. Interpreting answers to questions is always subjective and only as accurate as the interviewers' interpretations, recollections, and notes.

Identifying high performers through a résumé and a thorough interview is only part of the total selection process. You will also want to check their references. While many companies are now limiting responses to verifying the dates of employment and the position held, you do want to check references and get as much information as possible about the candidates' previous performances. References for the high performer in sales will often indicate that this person was incredible at the job, but not easy to work with.

Once you've identified your top candidates, you're ready to assess them and get results that give you perspectives that go beyond what you can determine from a résumé or in-person interview.

MOVING FORWARD

Having a simple and effective interview process that aligns with the technical skills, experience, soft skills, and problem solving skills that you are looking for in your top sales candidates will provide more candidates to choose from and better practices for screening and interviewing. You can narrow your search to the most qualified candidates using techniques for screening résumés and by using telephone screening.

The next chapter demonstrates how measuring the soft skills and problem-solving skills (combining a hiring process with assessments) creates a more effective hiring strategy. In step 3, assessing your top candidates, you'll learn how to apply the attributes by using the results to identify your top candidate's strengths and weaknesses.

Chapter

6

Step 4:
Assess Your
Top Candidates

No victor believes in chance.

—Friedrich Nietzsche, German Philosopher

CANDIDATE TESTING IS FAST BECOMING A STANDARD PART OF THE FINAL CANDIDATE selection process. While there are human factors involved in reviewing interview results, the assessment provides empirical results for comparing your final top candidates. It's important for legal reasons to use assessments after conducting the interviews and *never* for initial candidate screening.

In the same way you develop interview questions that cover many different aspects to determine a person's qualifications and fit for the position, you want an assessment that provides multiple perspectives, for example, a complete view of the candidate's competencies, critical thinking, and core values described in Chapter 4. You will also want an assessment that requires benchmarking, that is, identifying the soft skills and problem-solving skills required for the job. Having reports that make it easy to interpret results and compare multiple candidates is also important when considering an assessment system.

> **Be Sure to Use Validated Assessments**
>
> Look for a tool that has been validated for selection and development, conforms to the Equal Employment Opportunity Commission (EEOC) Guidelines, and provides the data to accurately assess your candidates.

Do not use profiling as a way to screen out candidates. Using a profiling tool as the *only* tool to screen candidates is prohibited in many states. Even if it weren't, you will need both the empirical and personal assessment perspectives to have a clear picture of how candidates fit within your organization and for the specific position.

So far you may have picked up on how assessments can enhance some of your hiring best practices, such as benchmarking. There are legal ramifications for using assessments inappropriately, but people also use the wrong assessments or use the results inappropriately. Why take the time and cost for assessing employees when it serves little or no purpose. The more you know about assessments, the more you can see their value and appreciate the correct application of their results.

Using assessments to make more informed hiring decisions is just one way to hire top sales performers. Becoming familiar with the various purposes of assessments will broaden your ability to apply assessments in all the different ways they can support you and your managers.

According to a Rocket-Hire survey conducted in 2006, 76 percent of all organizations use some type of preemployment assessment tool. Figure 6-1 shows the usage rates of the most common assessment tools.

APPLICATIONS FOR SALES

As you can see from Figure 6-1, there are many measurements for assessment tools. And there are numerous applications for using them. For hiring and developing sales talent, here are the primary ways we recommend using assessment:

- ◆ Profiling of sales jobs

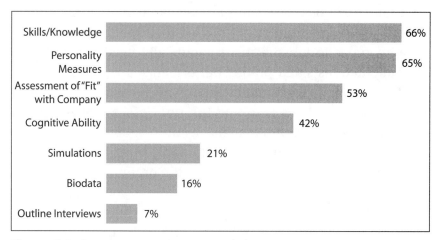

Figure 6-1. Assessment tool usage statistics

- Selection of sales candidates
- Customization of interview questions
- Creation of job descriptions
- Leadership training
- Measurement of job-relevant skills
- Identification of sales talent
- Development of sales talent
- Coaching
- Team building
- Talent research projects
- Group communication training
- Sales training
- Customer service training
- Succession planning

To be able to provide all the recommended services requires assessing the most important attributes for sales candidates in an ongoing employee assessment program. Determining employee abilities, soft skills, and problem solving skills will provide a pathway for developing a sales force with higher job satisfaction, longer-term commitment, and higher productivity.

Many types of assessments are available in the marketplace, ranging in quality from poorly crafted tools that take advantage of stereotypes to job-specific, scientifically validated tests and nonvalidated tests that predict performance outcomes.

The challenge for human resource professionals, sales managers, and executives is to find the right assessments to fulfill their purposes. Preemployment testing should serve as an opportunity to contribute to a sustainable business by identifying employees who will best fit with the organization and position. When times are tough, the talent pool widens and organizations are faced with even more choices. By understanding the ins and outs of testing and validation, executives, HR professionals, and anyone else responsible for the business of hiring have the opportunity to be successful in hiring a high-performing sales team.

STANDARDIZED WORKPLACE ASSESSMENTS FOR SALES

In some industries the U.S. government requires salespeople to be licensed. In others, licensing is controlled on a state-by-state basis. For example, real estate salespeople, insurance brokers, and financial planners who want to sell securities all must be licensed.

One strategy to boost an individual's sales is to obtain certification by completing an internship, coursework, or an examination. The logic is that those with certification are viewed as more informed and trusted in their field than those without. Many industries offer certification programs that are even company-specific. The pharmaceutical, communications, and computer industries all have certification programs for their sales and sales support people as well as their strategic third-party vendors.

All these methods provide hiring managers with some degree of certainty about how knowledgeable candidates are in their areas of expertise. Yet the vast majority of sales positions have no certification or licensing, and the content knowledge needed to perform comes from company-developed or on-the-job training. And generic sales training alone won't necessarily broaden an individual's capabilities. So to create a better fit between salespeople and the job, a variety of assessments have been devised that can identify a person's strengths and areas for improvement and provide specific areas for development. Understanding the different kinds offered and their intended uses can help you select the right assessment to fulfill your hiring and development needs.

CHOOSING ASSESSMENTS FOR SELECTING SALES CANDIDATES OR DEVELOPING YOUR SALES TALENT

Our research shows that the following soft skills and problem-solving skills are important components to measure in hiring and developing high-performing salespeople. Here's a brief overview of the assessment attributes we discuss in detail in the chapters that follow.

Competencies

Competency tests measure a candidate's knowledge of the specific skills required for a job. It's essential to know that the test you select to measure the competencies for the position you are hiring for only tests the competencies required for the job category and follows EEOC Guidelines. Otherwise, you can open yourself to discrimination suits. Make sure any assessment that you will use has been constructed in a way that meets the requisite guidelines. In addition to assessing your top candidates for making a better hiring decision, assessing job-related competencies can be used to help develop employees. Showing your employees their strengths and weaknesses in relation to what is required for the job will help them develop to their full potential.

Cognitive Skills

Assessment of cognitive ability reflects the ability to reason through and analyze complex problems, use insight to generate novel ideas and solutions, and effectively integrate abstract thinking with practical intelligence. Therefore, an individual's general cognitive ability can aid in predicting behaviors and performance related to job success.

There are three primary purposes that the results from a cognitive assessment can serve:

- Candidate selection
- Identification of gaps in an existing sales team
- Succession planning

Most cognitive assessments on the market analyze general intelligence rather than target job-related aspects. For a cognitive assessment to be used for job placement, all items measured should be business related and job relevant. That way you can correlate the candidates' results more closely to on-the-job performance. Selecting the right cognitive assessment tool will help to determine which candidates are more qualified or better on-the-job performers for a sales job.

Thinking Styles (for Developing Your Sales Talent)

A dimension that can also be measured is thinking style, which tells us how a person's mind works in regard to how the person solves problems and gathers and processes information and what kinds of information that person gravitates toward. These attributes, measured uniquely through the XC InSight System, were developed in conjunction with the entire program of assessments to provide a broad job-relevant measure of attributes. These thinking-style attributes are used exclusively to help individuals understand their strengths and weaknesses so managers can help them work toward their strengths and understand where they can work to improve.

Behavioral Assessment

People often confuse personality and behavioral assessments and try to use them interchangeably. In contrast to personality assessments, behavioral testing doesn't reveal core personality types; instead, it reveals how your personality responds to your environment. So personality is half the equation; the other half is how the personality responds to a particular situation. Personality and situation interact, and produce thoughts, feelings, and behaviors. Assessments that characterize personality type are only useful if people have a practical way to apply the information from their results to the work environment. You can't change your personality, but you can choose to change your behavior, the way that you respond to situations and to your environment. Personality begins with a unique genetic makeup and forms as a person has life experiences. Personality has many facets to it. For example, some people are extroverted and some people are introverted. We don't get to choose our personalities, and we cannot change them; so we say personality characteristics are hard-wired. They come out of how we were brought up, what we were taught in school, and what we have experienced; but at the same time, they are based in our original genetic predisposition.

Personality testing is commonly used inappropriately to assess job placement and candidate fit. There are a number of instruments for measuring personality. The most widely known is the Myers-Briggs Type Indicator. You can discover your personality type through assessment, but you can't change it. People tend to adapt to their surroundings, and a behavioral assessment will show how individuals adapt—how they work within situations; and so there is more to be gained from understanding how a person adapts and how their particular behaviors will fit within a particular job and environment.

Each person has a preferred style of giving and receiving information. The lack of understanding of these styles often causes delays, misconceptions, and even conflict. Discovering the differences and working with each individual's boundaries greatly smooths the flow of communication.

A major tool for learning about the differences in communication styles is behavioral profiling. Through behavioral profiling, you can learn the communication dos and don'ts for working effectively with your salespeople. You can learn the best way to motivate and coach each salesperson. It's helpful for salespeople to understand their preferred method of communication as well as to recognize the different styles for interacting with customers and prospects. Understanding these differences and ways to compensate for them is essential for developing your salespeople.

If you choose to look at a behavioral component as part of your hiring process for your salespeople, then use it only to determine how your candidate will fit into your organization and how you might coach, lead, and manage this individual if he or she becomes part of your team.

Core Values and Motivation

By understanding what drives and motivates a person in relation to the work environment, other team members, and the job, you will ensure a better fit. Someone who places a high value on adventure will be unhappy in a rote sales job where everything is predictable and unchanging. Someone who likes independence will be happiest in a sales job that may be virtual or requires little or no dependence on other sales team members.

Through an understanding of people's core values, hiring managers are provided with keen insight into the type of work and the work environment that is motivating to each person in candidate selection and the employee development process.

WHAT TO LOOK FOR WHEN SELECTING AN ASSESSMENT

All high-quality, well-constructed tests should have the following characteristics so the results can be put to their intended use.

Validity

Studies and research should be ongoing for the assessment and should show that the assessment measures what it is supposed to measure. For example, competencies assessment should report on an individual's level of competency for the skills the job requires. (Validity is explained in more detail later in the chapter.)

Reliability

The studies and research for the assessment during development and through ongoing studies should also show that the test results are accurate within an acceptable margin of error. (Reliability is explained in detail later in the chapter.)

Thoroughness

Length matters, and the assessment should ask enough questions so the results give a full picture of the candidate's ability, behavior, or whatever the assessment is measuring.

Objective Scoring

The assessment should provide a scoring system that eliminates human judgment to give you empirical results, the best kind of results for creating a true picture of a candidate's or employee's skills, competence, behavior, and so on.

Accuracy

The individual items in the assessment should be error free, without misspellings and without internal errors. They should be constructed according to sound psychometric principles. For example, incorrect choices in multiple-choice tests must be plausible, written with parallel structure, and similar enough to the correct answer but inarguably wrong.

Customization of Competencies

Assessments should allow for hiring managers and subject-matter experts to identify the specific job requirements so what is important and relevant is measured. This is an essential component for ensuring job relevance and administering an assessment that meets the EEOC Guidelines.

Up-to-Date and Relevant

Any assessment will become dated and irrelevant over time if not continually validated and modified to reflect our ever-changing work environment.

OTHER SELECTION CONSIDERATIONS

In addition to quality construction, there are other considerations for selecting assessments:

Easy Interpretation

The assessment should provide the results in a way that makes it easy to understand and apply in the real world. For example, the data should allow for clear comparisons among candidates.

Simple Administration

The tests should be easily administered in a way that doesn't favor one candidate or employee over another, and without the need for expensive equipment and or a long interpretation time.

Worldwide Access and Delivery

Having assessments that are readily available online anytime, anywhere, will make them easier to access and administer.

Multiple and Versatile Applications

Many assessments have only one application because the results can only be used for one purpose. Others report data that can be aggregated different ways, so there are many ways to use the results that can be applied in the real world. An assessment used for hiring can also help with integrating a new employee into the job, for example.

To get the best value for your investment of both time and money, be sure that the assessments you select report the results in as many useful ways as possible. Here are some examples of how results for a hiring assessment can be analyzed and interpreted to provide a wealth of information for multiple uses:

- The key qualities (talents) and experience that the potential hire needs to possess to be successful in the job
- A recommended fit for each sales candidate to more easily compare one candidate against the others in a hiring assessment

- Both summary reports and longer, detailed results
- Interview questions that hiring managers can ask sales candidates based on their lower-scoring items
- Reports that show how to coach, motivate, and lead each potential new hire

As you can see, picking the right assessments to give the results needed for making decisions can be complex.

LEGAL IMPLICATIONS OF HIRING ASSESSMENTS

While assessments are helpful for identifying job candidates, using assessments for selecting new hires can't be used in isolation. Each state has its own rules and criteria for the hiring process, but the Equal Employment Opportunity Commission Guidelines are clear that you can't use an online assessment tool as the sole screening process for candidates. It is imperative that you also include an in-person interview before any assessment takes place. Use assessments as part of your hiring process. Don't make them the process. Use them as a follow-up to in-person interviews to compare the top-quality candidates. To minimize your risk, be sure the assessments comply with the following recommendations:

- American Psychological Association Standards
- Society for Industrial/Organizational Psychology Principles
- EEOC Guidelines

Once you properly screen and interview a candidate to determine who are your top candidates, you are ready to administer an assessment. You must be sure that the assessments you use have been validated and you are using them according to the way and purpose for which they are intended.

Reliability and validity are two properties of assessments that are complex but important to understand because they'll tell you about the quality and usefulness of the assessments for hiring and developing salespeople.

Reliability

Reliability tells you how consistently an assessment measures what it says it measures. Reliability tells you if the results are dependable. If a person takes the same (or the equivalent) assessment over, the closer the second results are to the first, the greater the reliability. The more dependable and repeatable the results for an assessment, the more weight you can give them. Reliability is determined statistically. You will want to be sure that the level of reliability for assessments you choose is adequate. If you are using multiple assessments, check both the individual assessments and the combined results.

It's difficult for any assessment to have 100 percent reliability. There is a margin of error that's hard to avoid, and sometimes it has nothing to do with the assessment itself, but can be related to an adverse change in environment (an overheated room, for example); a change in the person's state such as alertness, motivation, or level of anxiety; or other factors external to the assessment that can affect the results. There are industry standards within which the reliability results should fall so you get useful results from an assessment.

In addition to reliability, you can look at the standard deviation, also called the standard error of measurement, which is derived statistically and tells you the range in which the test taker's true score lies. You may have noticed how the TV news will report voting exit polls within a margin of error. They are saying to the viewers that if the same polls were taken over, the results might not be exactly the same but they would be consistent within a certain range. The smaller the range, the more you tend to take the results seriously.

You should also know what studies were used to determine the reliability and whether the practices were statistically sound. Professionally developed assessments should provide this information.

Validity

Validity tells you how well the assessment correlates to what it purports to measure, for example, how well the results will predict on-the-job performance. Validity is the most important statistic to help you determine whether you are using the right assessment to meet your needs. Assessment instruments, like other tools, can be extremely helpful when used properly, but counterproductive when used inappropriately. Often, inappropriate use stems from not having a clear understanding of what you want to measure and why you want to measure it. Validity tells you what an assessment measures—for example, predicting how well someone will perform on the job. More important, validity tells you the degree to which you can draw specific conclusions or predictions based on a person's scores.

Validity is only relevant for a particular purpose in a particular situation. If you try to use an assessment for a different purpose than intended or haven't ensured that your situation is mapped to the intended situation, then the validity scores are irrelevant. Validity will tell you how useful the results are for your particular situation and purpose. Many methods are used to establish validity, and it's important to know the validity studies for any assessment tool you use follow all the industry guidelines and state-of-the-art research.

One important aspect of validation is job relatedness, so an assessment based on a job analysis and developed to measure on-the-job success for a particular position will be highly job related. The validation establishes the links between essential aspects of the job and the assessment tool. For example, if you want to use an assessment for hiring salespeople, your validity will be higher for an assessment developed specifically for sales candidates, especially if you can customize it for your particular sales position. To be valid, the assessment must have a high correlation to the job performance.

Adverse Impact

The general purpose of employment laws and regulations is to prohibit unfair discrimination in employment and provide equal employment opportunity for all. One of the basic principles of the *Uniform Guidelines on Employee Selection Procedures* published in 1978 is that it's unlawful to use a test or selection procedure that creates adverse impact, unless justified. *Adverse impact* occurs when there is a substantially different rate of selection in hiring, promotion, or other employment decisions that works to the disadvantage of members of a race, sex, or ethnic group. A well-constructed assessment will test for adverse impact and revise or eliminate the items that any of these groups do more poorly on than the whole target group. Like reliability, many factors affect an assessment's adverse impact.

Different approaches exist that can determine whether adverse impact has occurred. Statistical techniques may provide information regarding the degree to which the use of a test results in adverse impact. It's essential to use assessments that have been tested for adverse impact.

More Information

It's important to measure multiple areas when assessing your sales candidates. Someone who scores high on a competency test that predicts successful on-the-job performance might not score well on a cognitive test that predicts overall intelligence. On the other hand, someone who scores high on the cognitive test and high on the competency test might reveal during an interview poor face-to-face social skills. Using multiple tactics for hiring provides the best opportunity for determining the best fit.

For any assessment you choose, be sure that the reliability, validity, and adverse impact procedures, studies, and results are documented in accordance with professional and legal guidelines. The above summaries describing adverse impact, validity, and reliability have been taken in part from *Testing and Assessment: An Employer's Guide to Good Practices*, prepared by the Skills Assessment and Analysis Program in the U.S. Department of Labor, Employment and Training Administration, Office of Policy and Research, published in 2000. This guide provides more detail on interpreting the statistics for validity, reliability, and adverse impact as well as the appropriate uses and interpretation of assessment results.

CASE STUDY: A TOP-CANDIDATE ASSESSMENT

Eva Rios is looking for a sales account executive who can hit the ground running. Eva is a sales director in the medical field and works closely with Dana Shepherd, a marketing manager responsible for their company's largest brand segment with many different products. Dana is responsible for the marketing budget. She provides the marketing brochures, samples, and other promotional materials to Eva for the sales force, often in connection with an extensive marketing campaign. Eva's job is to make sure that her salespeople focus on a specific product as marketing campaigns launch and that they get the projected sales return on the marketing investment.

Eva needs salespeople who can juggle working with multiple products and adapt quickly to switching product focus while learning new pitches and figuring out how to sell into many different customer environments. She needs salespeople who can develop rapport with the gatekeepers in order to have an opportunity for face time with their customers, who happen to be very busy physicians. She needs salespeople who are accustomed to being flexible, seizing the opportunity, and making sure that they get to talk with the doctors. When the salespeople get the time, they will have a short window to establish rapport and pitch their products, so they have to communicate effectively, analyze a situation, come up with different solutions to a problem quickly, and gain buy-in. These salespeople have to be achievement oriented and goal focused.

Working with physicians, they will need to exude confidence and relish the challenge of influencing these knowledgeable customers. Eva and others familiar with the job requirements completed the job profile for this position to identify the 3 Cs: Competencies, Critical Thinking, and Core Values.

Eva has been screening candidates by reading résumés,

conducting telephone interviews, and then doing a follow-up in-person interview. Lee Washington is one of her top candidate picks. His résumé shows strong sales experience, with a steady to moderately fast rise in the ranks and level of responsibility. In both the telephone and in-person interviews, he demonstrated strong communication skills. He presented himself with confidence on the phone; and in person, he exuded confidence, one of her primary requirements. He impressed Eva with his assertiveness and competitiveness in both his answers to her questions and those he asked.

So Eva invited Lee to take the XC InSight Assessment. Before meeting with Lee again, she begins to review his results. First she looks at the Candidate Assessment Report, which provides a thorough review of Lee's results. Then she looks at the Candidate Summary Report, which gives her an easy way to collect the positive areas of fit between Lee and the position as well as to make notes of areas she will need to explore and consider further.

Summary of Results

The first section that Eva looks at is the results summary. The assessment results give her an instant picture of the job-candidate fit, and the summarizing statements clearly interpret the data for her.

High	Scores greater than 79	
Moderate	Scores between 40 and 79	
Low	Scores below 40	
Overall Rank	**Competency**	**Score**
1	Seizes opportunities	97
2	Demonstrates flexibility/resilience	99
3	Builds customer loyalty	95
4	Gains buy-in	99

Table 6-1. Candidate assessment results summary

Overall Rank	Competency	Score
5	Maintains endurance	97
6	Communicates articulately	99
7	Develops and maintains relationships	96
Overall Rank	Critical Thinking	Score
1	Reasons logically	59
2	Reasons numerically	19
3	Reasons verbally	30
Overall Rank	Values	Score
1	Achievement	97
2	Power and overt influence	53
3	Adventure	92

Table 6-1. Candidate assessment results summary (continued)

Competencies: All of the candidate's top seven competencies score as a high fit for the job.

Critical thinking: Reasons Logically scores in the average range and comes out as a moderate fit. Two of the three critical thinking areas (Reasons Numerically and Reasons Verbally) score in the below-average range and come out as a low fit.

Core Values: Two of the top three values of the job profile (Achievement and Adventure) come out as a high fit for the job.

Table 6-2. Candidate summary

From the information in the summaries, the candidate appears to have the competence to perform the job, as all seven competencies are strong. The report on his values and motivators confirms her impressions from her interviews that he is achievement motivated and has a strong competitive drive.

There seems to be a question, however, of whether he has the requisite critical thinking skills. She realizes she needs to know more about this candidate before determining if he is the best person for the job.

So next she looks more closely at the competency profile (shown in Figure 6-2).

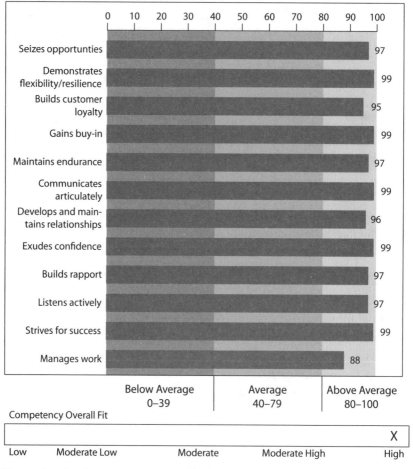

Figure 6-2. Lee's competency profile

Competency Profile

Lee scores in the above-average range in all the 12 competencies defined as most important for the job. In particular for selling into physicians, being able to seize an opportunity is crucial, as are gaining buy-in and exuding confidence, which are Lee's top three competencies. Table 6-3 shows the candidate's areas of strength.

Strengths

Seizes Opportunities: Takes initiative for success and anticipates obstacles.

Demonstrates Flexibility/Resilience: Anticipates change and develops contingency plans.

Builds Customer Loyalty and Develops and Maintains Relationships: Makes customers a top priority and builds and maintains long-term relationships with customers.

Gains Buy-In: Looks for alternatives to find win-win solutions and then negotiates deliverables and schedules.

Maintains Endurance: Establishes and maintains a productive pace while working. Demonstrates persistence and refusal to give up when faced with obstacles and sets the pace.

Communicates Articulately: Demonstrates an ability to speak clearly and concisely, and demonstrates skill in using expressiveness to convey important points in verbal communications.

Exudes Confidence: Demonstrates adequate knowledge and confidence in his ability to perform the job.

Builds Rapport: Makes a good first impression and establishes rapport easily with customers.

Listens Actively: Listens carefully to others' needs, concerns, and perspectives. Asks clarifying questions to enhance understanding.

Strives for Success: Demonstrates a strong drive to achieve organizational goals.

Manages Work: Sets priorities, monitors work progress, and follows up to meet deadlines and keep projects on track.

Table 6-3. Lee's Areas of Strength

Critical Thinking Profile

Looking at the critical thinking profile, shown in Figure 6-3, Eva had more concerns.

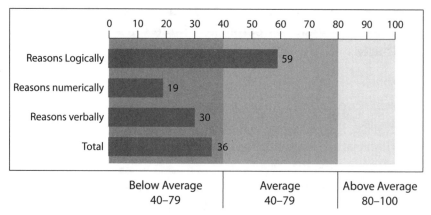

Figure 6-3. Lee's critical thinking profile

Lee scored in the average range in Reasons Logically. He will be effective at dealing with multiple issues and demands and will use logic and reasoning to identify the strengths and weaknesses of alternative solutions, conclusions, or approaches to problems.

But he scored in the below-average range for Reasons Numerically and Reasons Verbally. This means he may find it more difficult to analyze data, draw conclusions, and reason based on numbers.

He also scored in the below-average range for Reasons Verbally. He will have difficulty identifying themes and thinking on an abstract level.

When Eva returns to look at Lee's résumé, she can see that in past positions he was usually working with a single product. Lee's ability to juggle many products was probably not tested in his previous positions as they would be in her organization.

Core Values and Motivation Profile

Eva continues to review the summary by looking at Lee's values (Figure 6-4 and Table 6-4).

From Lee's values she can see why Lee impressed her during the interview as someone who is highly competitive and achievement and goal oriented.

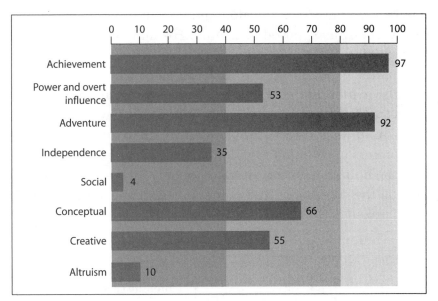

Figure 6-4. Lee's core values and motivation profile

Two of the top three values of the job profile score highest for this candidate

He will be motivated by achieving challenging goals. (High Achievement)

He will also be motivated by competition and enjoys taking calculated risks. He likes to tackle new challenges and can work well under pressure. (High Adventure)

Table 6-4. Lee's top-scoring values

Behavioral Profile

While the behaviors aren't a measure of how well Lee will perform on the job, Eva looks at that section next because it will tell her how he will fit into her overall organization and how she must prepare to manage him. (Chapter 10 explains behaviors in detail.)

As Figure 6-5 shows, Lee scored high in impacting (I), which indicates he will focus on people. Building relationships will be important to him. Because he is so people focused, he will be a verbal communicator, and he will prefer to communicate verbally as opposed to writing. His high impacting (I) and high driving (D) scores indicate that he will move quickly. He will prefer quick responses and will not favor long, detailed reports or presentations. His low score in supporting (S) indicates that he prefers variety and change. His low score in contemplating (C) indicates that he does not like a lot of structure and prefers to work independently. Eva will need to make sure that she helps Lee to concentrate not only on the end result but also on the details and the process. Lee's behavioral profile is summarized in Table 6-5.

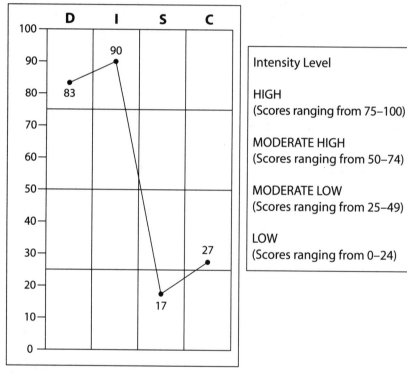

Figure 6-5. Lee's behavioral profile

What can we say about how Lee will be for Eva to manage?

What Eva Has Learned

Having the candidate profile gives Eva some crucial informa-

DISC Summary

Characteristics: Lee's style is typically seen as persuasive, independent, and action oriented. He tends to be competitive, decisive, energetic, and tenacious. He also tends to be fast paced and urgent and determined to push for results.

Overextensions: Because Lee has a high sense of urgency, he can become impatient if others don't move at his pace. He thrives on change and variety, so he may take on too many projects or tasks in a short time. He may not convey adequate detail when communicating and can be a situational listener. While he is comfortable in a crisis, he may be too reactive in situations that call for a more well-thought-out, detailed plan.

Ideal Work Setting: An environment that allows him to be efficient and results focused and where he can use his people skills to influence and drive toward goals is ideal. Challenging assignments are important, as someone with Lee's style gets bored quickly with routine tasks. He prefers freedom from excessive detail and supervision.

Table 6-5. Lee's behavioral profile summary

tion that she might not otherwise have gleaned from Lee's résumé or the interviews.

From the Candidate Assessment Report, she has questions for her next interview with Lee to figure out what kind of support he will need to develop his organizational skills:

- What steps have you taken to be more organized with regard to your work?
- Describe a time when you had several projects due at once. How did you approach this workload, and what was the outcome?
- Describe a time when you failed to meet a deadline. Why did this happen? What were the repercussions?

MOVING FORWARD

Not all assessments are validated for hiring purposes. You will want to choose a tool that meets EEOC guidelines and other hiring standards. Beyond their immediate uses, assessment results can help in many other ways. Rather than serving the employer, the candidates can benefit from the results by knowing areas for improvement and managers will benefit because they can provide more directed support in those areas to the employee. In addition to understanding the correct uses for the specific types of assessments, knowing all of the different applications for results gives you a greater return on your investment.

The next chapter shows how important it is to use assessments that measure multiple areas and how you can use this information to make your hiring decisions as well as compare your top candidates.

Chapter

7 How to Compare Your Top Candidates

There are so many who can figure costs, and so few who can measure value.

—Author Unknown

SEEKING VP OF SALES

Don Manning is the senior VP of human resources for Sun Company, a multimedia company located in a major metropolitan market. Don is in the middle of a candidate search for a vice president of advertising sales, someone who can develop and execute sales strategies, put the systems and people in place to execute, and expand the company's client base and increase market share. The successful candidate will report to the president. Sun is looking for someone who can bring original ideas, execute the new programs, and lead in a challenging environment. The VP will also need to participate on the executive team and develop revenue growth strategies.

Sun has hired and lost two VPs in the past three years, both of whom had disappointing performances. The past two candidates failed to develop their sales organization into one that responds quickly to new opportunities and adapts to new media. Consequently they missed annual revenue targets. There is a lot riding on bringing in a candidate who will be successful in the changing Sun environment. Sun needs someone who has the skills to execute in the short term but also provide a long-term strategy for growth. Here is the complete job description based on interviews with managers and people successful in the position, the performance standards, and the job benchmark.

Job Description

JOB TITLE: Senior Vice President of Media Sales

Reports to: The President/CEO of Media Sales

POSITION

The Vice President/Media Sales is responsible for building a high-performing multimedia sales organization by recruiting and developing talented sales professionals and by developing and executing sales strategies, systems, and plans to ensure attainment of the company's sales goals for revenue, client base, and market share growth. As a member of the executive management team of the Sun Company, the position participates in the creation and execution of the company's vision, strategy, priorities, and overall operating plans.

The scope of responsibility for this position includes planning, managing, directing, and controlling all sales division operations, functions, and staff serving Sun Company. The position is accountable for over $450 million in advertising revenue and over $40 million of annual operating expense. It has four direct reports (three sales directors and one advertising operations manager) and indirectly manages over 200 employees.

SALES AND INDUSTRY EXPERIENCE

At least 10 years progressive experience in media sales, building and leading successful sales organizations, with at least 5 years in a senior sales management position; media, advertising, marketing, or consumer products background preferred.

EDUCATIONAL BACKGROUND AND TECHNICAL SKILLS

Training: BA or BS in business, marketing, or other related discipline; MBA or other master's degree desirable.

SUPERVISION EXERCISED

This position directly supervises director and managerial-level staff and indirectly supervises the entire sales division.

KEY RESPONSIBILITIES

Leadership Skills

◆ Encourage, direct, and reinforce sales division management and staff to support and align activities and behaviors with the company's vision, values, and strategic priorities, i.e., leadership by example.

◆ Lead and direct employees and activities in the marketplace in a manner consistent with company values.

◆ Build and lead a high-performing sales team of service professionals; one that provides superior performance with a strong focus on execution and results, a high sense of urgency, and client satisfaction.

◆ Lead and promote innovation and sales initiatives that support the company's product portfolio and enhance sales opportunities and revenue and share growth.

◆ Lead and promote continuous improvements in sales processes and systems, products, and pricing that support growth and profitability goals; this may include elimination of products or services.

Managerial Skills

◆ Strategically plan, allocate, and deploy sales resources to optimize sales effectiveness; develop revenue forecasts and projections for the division and each sales team.

◆ Achieve/exceed company goals for revenue and market share growth. Achieve organization goals by hiring/retaining qualified and talented sales management and staff and installing effective sales training/development programs and pay-for-performance compensation plans.

◆ Build and maintain strong, effective sales systems, procedures, and customer service programs to sustain growth and retention of media clients and client satisfaction at all levels.

◆ Identify and make improvements/changes to personnel, processes, compensation, functions, and structures to improve sales effectiveness and other facets of selling and service.

- Proactively engage in the development and launch of new-product initiatives to capitalize on market opportunities and maintain competitive advantage.
- Monitor and track changes in the market, industry, and competitor activities and develop timely and appropriate responses to ensure and maintain a strong market position.

JOB-RELATED QUALIFICATIONS
Knowledge of:
- Strategic selling strategies to grow revenue client base and market share.
- Customer relationship and account management strategies to retain/increase share of client spending.
- Sales recruiting, talent assessment, training, coaching, development, and compensation strategies.
- Regulations, laws, and requirements of the industry as they pertain to advertising, pricing, and antitrust.

Skill to:
- Lead the sales division in continuous improvement processes to enhance sales effectiveness.
- Forecast revenue and sales force performance trends and determine appropriate courses of action.

After reviewing résumés, conducting telephone screenings, and interviewing eight candidates who met the education, job experience, and preliminary interview criteria, the hiring team identified three top candidates. Now the final decision lies in the hands of the company's hiring team and ultimately the company president. The hiring team is ready to compare its top candidates to the Job Profile Report.

CANDIDATE ASSESSMENT RESULTS

In the past at this stage of the hiring process, which followed the in-person interview, Sun compared the final round of candidates and based its hiring decision for the most part on technical skills, experience, and gut instinct.

In this latest candidate search, from the preliminary résumé screening, recommendations, and interviews, the candidates appear to be very close in the job qualifications and the way they present themselves personally. For the first time, Sun has added an assessment component to its hiring practices. Don and his team are hopeful that using the XC InSight Candidate Assessment and the XC InSight Multiple Candidate Comparison Report will provide better information about the candidates and reveal who will be the best candidate. They can't afford another mistake.

A NEW APPROACH

The comparison report in the XC InSight System provides candidates' skills and aptitudes in comparison to the Job Profile Report (benchmark). The report shows both their individual strengths and weakness in relation to the Job Profile Report as well as in relation to each other.

REVIEWING THE SUMMARY REPORT

The purpose of a multiple candidate report is to provide a high-level view of each candidate in relation to the important attributes of the benchmarked job. So it's a high-level view of the top seven competencies, as well as the core values and critical thinking (cognitive) skills important to the position (as defined by the hiring managers by using the XC InSight System). With this report you can look at how the candidates scored relative to one another within the three areas.

Let's meet our three candidates and see how they compare overall in the three areas of the assessment by reviewing the Multiple Candidate Comparison Report.

Summary Overview

The chart in Table 7-1 provides an overview of the candidates' scores for three of the assessment areas that were the results of the Job Profile Report: competencies, critical thinking, and core values.

Looking at the results of the multicandidate reports in detail

High	Scores greater than 79		
Moderate	Scores between 40 and 79		
Low	Scores below 40		

Overall Rank	Competency	1	2	3
1	Seizes opportunities	90	90	55
2	Demonstrates flexibility/resilience	93	89	59
3	Builds customer loyalty	99	83	93
4	Gains buy-in	98	89	93
5	Maintains endurance	99	83	83
6	Communicates articulately	78	59	59
7	Develops and maintains relationships	85	34	64
Overall Rank	Critical Thinking	6	7	8
1	Reasons logically	50	33	9
2	Reasons numerically	44	92	4
3	Reasons verbally	50	29	50
Overall Rank	Values	6	7	8
1	Achievement	92	99	44
2	Power and overt influence	5	15	88
3	Adventure	85	43	77

Candidate 1: Michael Taylor
Candidate 2: Robert Thomas
Candidate 3: Joanne Zimmerman

Table 7-1. Multiple candidate summary

provides deeper insight into each candidate's strengths and weaknesses. It's important to remember that this is one part of the hiring decision, as the interviews were extensive, with targeted competency and core values questions. Don and his team can also use the data to decide whether they need to open their search again. They cannot afford to make another hiring mistake. The future of the company is at stake. Here are the detailed reports on the competencies grouped in order-of-fit importance and the candidates' capabilities according to the assessment results.

Candidate 1: Michael Taylor

Competency Comparison

Michael Taylor scored in the following fit range for the top seven competencies, critical thinking, and the top three core values in the job profile:

High Fit:

◆ *Communicates Articulately.* Will demonstrate the ability to present messages and information in a clear and concise manner. Will communicate with enthusiasm and generate excitement when stating an opinion or making a point.

◆ *Develops and Applies Strategy.* Considers strategic issues in making decisions and proposes innovative strategies. Translates broad goals into actionable tactics and objectives to support the organization's vision.

◆ *Establishes Credibility.* Accepts responsibility for opinions and mistakes and models and inspires integrity. Will honor commitments, and openly expresses opinions and motives. Actions and words are aligned.

◆ *Exudes Executive Presence.* Will appear confident, self-assured, and unflappable. Remains poised and unwavering when faced with difficult challenges. Leads by example and will demonstrate how organizational goals are compatible with his individual goals.

◆ *Leads Courageously.* Is at ease making decisions and will take a stand on tough issues even when others disagree. Proactively drives ideas and champions organizational initiatives.

◆ *Seizes Opportunities.* Will take ownership and initiative for his success and will anticipate obstacles. Able to stay focused without external supervision or direction.

Moderate Fit:

◆ *Listens Actively.* Waits patiently to allow others to express their views. Considers others' viewpoints and uses open-ended questions to initiate discussions.

Critical Thinking Comparison

◆ **Reasons Logically** (moderate fit). Will exhibit some level of ability in dealing with multiple issues and demands and will use logic and reasoning to identify the strengths and weaknesses of alternative solutions, conclusions, or approaches to problems.

◆ **Reasons Verbally** (moderate fit). Will demonstrate some ability to think constructively, identify themes, and think on an abstract level.

◆ **Reasons Numerically** (moderate fit). Will exhibit a good ability to analyze data, draw conclusions, and reason based on numbers.

Values Comparison

◆ **Achievement** (high fit). Will be strongly motivated by achieving challenging goals.

◆ **Social** (low fit). Will not be motivated by developing relationships and interacting with and helping others. Will focus less on social interaction and may enjoy assignments that can be completed individually.

◆ **Conceptual** (high fit). Will be strongly motivated by work that is mentally stimulating and requires a high level of mental ability. Likes to be seen as an expert, enjoys solving complex problems, and seeks out learning opportunities to keep an active mind.

Candidate 2: Robert (Rob) Thomas

Competency Comparison

Rob Thomas scored in the following fit range for the top seven competencies in the job profile:

High Fit:

◆ **Communicates Articulately.** Will demonstrate the ability to present messages and information in a clear and concise manner. Will communicate with enthusiasm and generate excitement when stating an opinion or making a point.

◆ **Develops and Applies Strategy.** Considers strategic issues in making decisions and proposes innovative strategies. Translates broad goals into actionable tactics and objectives to support the organization's vision.

- **Establishes Credibility.** Accepts responsibility for opinions and mistakes and models and inspires integrity. Will honor commitments, and openly expresses opinions and motives. Actions and words are aligned.
- **Exudes Executive Presence.** Will appear confident, self-assured, and unflappable. Remains poised and unwavering when faced with difficult challenges. Leads by example and will demonstrate how organizational goals are compatible with his individual goals.
- **Leads Courageously.** Is at ease making decisions and will take a stand on tough issues even when others disagree. Proactively drives ideas and champions organizational initiatives.

Moderate Fit:
- **Listens Actively.** Waits patiently to allow others to express their views. Considers others' viewpoints and uses open-ended questions to initiate discussions.

Low Fit:
- **Seizes Opportunities.** Can struggle with taking initiative for success, creating contingency plans and anticipating obstacles. May need more direct supervision to stay focused.

Critical Thinking Comparison
- **Reasons Logically** (low fit). May struggle in dealing with multiple issues and demands. May be more inclined to use emotion versus logic and reasoning to identify the strengths and weaknesses of alternative solutions, conclusions, or approaches to problems.
- **Reasons Verbally** (high fit). Will demonstrate a strong ability to think constructively, identify themes, and think on an abstract level.
- **Reasons Numerically** (low fit). Will find it more difficult to analyze data, draw conclusions, and reason based on numbers.

Values Comparison
- **Achievement** (high fit). Will be strongly motivated by achieving challenging goals.
- **Social** (low fit). Will not be motivated by developing relationships and interacting with and helping others. Will focus less on social interaction and may enjoy assignments that can be completed individually.

- **Conceptual** (moderate fit). Will be motivated by work that is mentally stimulating and may like to be seen as an expert in some situations. Will enjoy a job that allows for continual learning opportunities.

Candidate 3: Joanne Zimmerman

Competency Comparison

Joanne Zimmerman scored in the following fit range for the top seven competencies in the job profile:

High Fit:

- **Communicates Articulately.** Will demonstrate the ability to present messages and information in a clear and concise manner. Will communicate with enthusiasm and generate excitement when stating an opinion or making a point.
- **Exudes Executive Presence.** Will appear confident, self-assured, and unflappable. Remains poised and unwavering when faced with difficult challenges. Leads by example and will demonstrate how organizational goals are compatible with her individual goals.
- **Leads Courageously.** Is at ease making decisions and will take a stand on tough issues even when others disagree. Proactively drives ideas and champions organizational initiatives.

Moderate Fit:

- **Develops and Applies Strategy.** At times, will consider strategic issues in making decisions. Will exhibit some ability to translate broad goals into actionable tactics and objectives to support the organization's vision.
- **Establishes Credibility.** Will present information positively and will openly discuss negatives. Willing to accept responsibility for mistakes. Does not embellish the facts but at times may paint a more optimistic picture to gain others' support.
- **Listens Actively.** Waits patiently to allow others to express their views. Considers others' viewpoints and uses open-ended questions to initiate discussions.
- **Seizes Opportunities.** At times, can struggle with taking initiative for success, creating contingency plans, and anticipating obstacles. May need some direction to stay focused.

Critical Thinking Comparison

♦ *Reasons Logically* (low fit). May struggle in dealing with multiple issues and demands. May be more inclined to use emotion versus logic and reasoning to identify the strengths and weaknesses of alternative solutions, conclusions, or approaches to problems.

♦ *Reasons Verbally* (low fit). Will have difficulty identifying themes and thinking on an abstract level.

♦ *Reasons Numerically* (moderate fit). Will exhibit a good ability to analyze data, draw conclusions, and reason based on numbers.

Values Comparison

♦ *Achievement* (moderate fit)—Will be motivated by achieving challenging goals.

♦ *Social* (high fit). Will be strongly motivated by developing relationships and interacting with and helping others.

♦ *Conceptual* (moderate fit). Will be motivated by work that is mentally stimulating and may like to be seen as an expert in some situations. Will enjoy a job that allows for continual learning opportunities.

In addition to competencies, critical thinking, and core values, understanding how a candidate will fit within your organization can also have value.

BEHAVIORAL-STYLE COMPARISON

A comparison of behavioral styles is not part of the job profile or benchmark report, and the behavioral-styles analysis will not predict who will be successful or unsuccessful on the job, but does provide an indication of how a person will approach his or her work. Behavioral tendencies should not be used to make hiring decisions. The way a person approaches vital tasks has implications for how that person will fit within an organization or team.

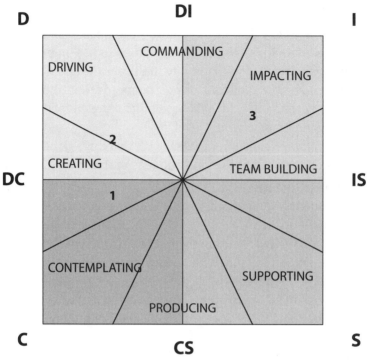

Figure 7-1. Candidates' team quadrant

Team Quadrant Descriptors

Driving – D
Direct, Tenacious, Bottom-Line Oriented, Results Focused, Visionary, Creative

Commanding – DI
Independent, Persuasive, Competitive, Innovative, Enthusiastic, Urgent

Impacting – I
Outgoing, Verbal, Trusting, Optimistic, People Oriented, Confident

Teambuilding – IS
Team Oriented, Warm, Supportive, Sensitive, Persistent, Easy-Going

Supporting – S
Logical, Cooperative, Steady, Consistent, Modest, Dependable

Producing – CS
Amiable, Self-Controlled, Systematic, Reflective, Thorough, Conscientious

Contemplating – C
Detailed, Quality Oriented, Perfectionist, Diplomatic, Accurate, Conservative

Creating – DC
Factual, Forceful, Impulsive, Systematic, Creative, Analytical
Following is the candidate that scores in the Driving segment on the quadrant: Candidate 2, Rob Thomas scores in the driving segment.

Descriptors
Direct, tenacious, bottom-line oriented, results focused, visionary, creative

Following is the candidate that scores in the Driving segment on the quadrant: Candidate 2, Rob Thomas scores in the driving segment.

Strengths of This Style
Will tend to focus on overcoming obstacles and will take on difficult problems with no fear. Is willing to lead results and is a fast decision maker.

Impacting – I
Following is the candidate that scores in the Impacting segment on the quadrant: Candidate 3, Joanne Zimmerman scores in the impacting segment.

Descriptors
Outgoing, verbal, trusting, optimistic, people oriented, confident

Strengths of This Style
Tendency to make a good first impression and is motivating to others. Builds rapport easily with others and is energetic and quick to act.

SUMMARY

A multiple candidate report compares the candidates with the Job Profile Report (benchmarked job) in the XC InSight System so that hiring managers can compare candidates against the competencies, core values, and critical thinking (cognitive) skills important to the job. The high-level view shows their relative areas of strength and fit with the soft skills and problem-skills required for superior performance in the job. Using an assessment report to compare the candidates is only one component of the final selection process and should be used to help you get a better picture of the soft and thinking skills for your top candidates. In addition to measuring soft skills and problem solving skills, you need to consider each candidate's technical skills and experience in combination with this information before making a hiring decision.

MOVING FORWARD

As you can see from this case study, measuring soft skills and problem-solving skills (in addition to experience and technical skills) provides you with valuable insights that enable you to compare the top candidates before you make your final selection. Looking at which candidates have the best fit overall, or in specific areas that your benchmark tells you are most important for success in the job, can confirm empirically what you've discovered in interviews and offer new perspectives.

Using assessment tools designed to provide results that help you decide the best fit for your position is often viewed as the final step in your hiring strategy, but that's only the beginning. With the right kind of assessment system, you will also have results so you understand potential growth opportunities for your new hire. Hiring is incomplete until your employee is integrated into your company with clear expectations and a work environment that creates the best fit and support for success on the job. The next chapter shows you how to create an employee development plan based on assessment results.

Chapter

8

Step 5: Develop Your Sales Talent

Every sale has five basic obstacles: no need, no money, no hurry, no desire, no trust.

—Zig Ziglar

WHEN YOU CHOOSE TO USE AN ASSESSMENT TO ASSIST YOU IN THE HIRING PROCESS for salespeople, make sure that once the candidate is hired, the assessment results can be used to help managers develop their new hires, as well. The hiring process won't be complete until you have a fully oriented, integrated employee with a clear development plan. After the expense of recruiting and hiring, you'll want to ensure you've made a sound investment by being able to use the assessment data to create a clear plan of action to engage and hold your new hire accountable.

The sooner you set expectations and create a road map by creating development plans for your employees, the more likely you are to have employees who are productive in the best way to support and grow your business. That isn't the only benefit. There are three primary reasons to create individual development plans for managing performance. Such a plan will:

1. Set expectations for performance. A plan gives employees clear expectations for their results. Statements in writing mean there is a greater likelihood of meeting or exceeding expectations. Having clear goals makes them more achievable.
2. Create a coaching document and put a process in place with a road map for advancement and a schedule to review progress, which holds managers accountable for providing ongoing feedback.
3. Create a benchmark that shows growth, improvement, or the lack of progress against goals. This benchmark will assist you in developing your sales professionals at all levels. Creating a record of improvement, or the lack of, will make it easier to adjust the job fit for the employees and to make decisions in a more timely way about where you want to invest in developing employees.

Development plans show what employees can do to grow and develop, to advance, to become more valued, and to be more satisfied in their work. Development plans also point out what kind of support and assistance they will need to get where they are going faster. As important as assessment is for hiring, using assessments to develop your employees is a worthwhile investment.

Once you've mastered the art of creating development plans for your salespeople, you'll want to create plans for your teams. Having an assessment system that enables you to use the data you've collected for the individual team members in a way that allows for further examination within teams extends your investment. By looking at the strengths and weaknesses of your teams you will be able to identify:

♦ Gaps in talent for future hiring
♦ Adjustments you can make across teams to more effectively use the salespeople you have
♦ Areas for team development

This can also be used to assess and integrate new teams acquired through mergers or acquisitions.

Many companies tie development to performance appraisal. While it's true you need to set expectations before you can identify areas for growth, employee development is an ongoing process. Reviews should be scheduled as often as needed according to the support, advancement, and abilities of each employee. Using assessments allows you to identify your top talent, and development is all about investing in your high potentials. Those whom you have identified for promotion, who have growth potential, and who are upwardly mobile are the ones you want to invest your money, time, and effort in developing.

By starting with an assessment upon hiring, you are in a position to offer goals and areas for improvement to set expectations to determine what you will measure. Each job and organization will evaluate and measure its employees using a variety of tools. Some of the most common include:

- Biannual or annual performance standards/reviews/appraisals: These usually include quantitative and qualitative sections where both the employee and manager have opportunities to make remarks. They state expectations and goals. The employee's performance is measured against these goals at the end of the time period. Traditionally, these appraisals are directly tied to annual bonuses or pay increases.
- Budget and quota measurements: These include measuring a person's performance against budget expectations and quotas. Employees are evaluated based on how well they perform, and rewards are directly tied to performance.

Regardless of how you choose to evaluate employees, using a development plan customized for each individual will make the performance evaluation process easier and fairer and offer ongoing opportunities to provide coaching and feedback not only at performance review time. It also reduces the risk of surprise in the results for the employees.

The manager and employee will work on the development plan together, but the more involved the employee is in determining the areas to work on, the more committed that individual will be to accomplishing the goals. The objective is to create an environment that encourages ongoing feedback from managers, which will help employees advance more quickly, achieve more, and avoid unnecessary problems and setbacks.

LEE WASHINGTON'S DEVELOPMENT PLAN

In the hiring case study presented in Chapter 6, we met Lee Washington. His hiring manager, Eva Rios, compared Lee's results with those of the other top candidates. She found that his competencies, critical thinking skills, and core values were the best match for the position among the choices and hired him. From the results of his assessment, his hiring manager was aware of areas for development without having to conduct an additional assessment. Because the hiring assessment was so closely tied to the job competencies, critical thinking, core values, and about Lee's behavioral style, it was easy to use the data to create a development plan for Lee once he was hired. The result is information that his new manager can use to coach him from the start, his first week on the job, giving him feedback in areas to help him be successful. With the initial investment for a hiring assessment, Eva learned she could provide Lee with support in the following areas:

- Coach him to summarize key points with customers before moving on to a new topic
- Provide support and help him prioritize when faced with competing issues and demands
- Help him practice patience
- Help him to create a structured plan for how he'll achieve his goals
- Coach him on improving his awareness of the body language that others project

- Help him to avoid procrastinating until the pressure is on so that he can avoid crisis situations

One mistake many managers make, often because they use poorly designed development plan templates, is to take on too many challenges at once. Keep the plan as simple as possible. Identify a combined total of two or three measurable objectives within the following three job-related categories:

Professional development objectives focus on the employee's career growth. Examples include attending classes, seminars, or workshops or participating in on-the-job training or self-study programs (e.g., books, cassette tapes, videos, CBTs, or web-based training).

Performance objectives are intended to help the employee improve personal aspects of his or her performance, behavior, or conduct. Examples of task-oriented performance goals are improving computer proficiency, time management, or presentation skills. Or the employee can focus on correcting behavioral problems that negatively impact group morale, job performance, or job satisfaction. Examples of such goals are developing conflict resolution or stress reduction techniques and building collaborative coworker relationships. As with professional development goals, effective performance objectives are well defined, are measurable, and are clearly linked to specific job-related outcomes.

Project objectives are specific assignments to participate in or manage ongoing or future projects. When setting project-oriented goals, outline the scope of the role the employee is to play, list resources and completion time frame, and define the desired result.

Components of an Effective Objective

Objectives must be ones the employee has agreed to accomplish within a specified time. The goals should be challenging but attainable and should be specific. Identify everything that both the employee and manager need to provide to accomplish the goals as an objective. Each objective should have four parts:

1. State the desired achievement for task mastery or improved behavior.
2. Define the applicability of each goal to the sales job function.
3. Specify the method of learning.
4. State the time frame for achievement.

Based on his hiring assessment results, here are the three most important competencies for Lee to work on:

- Strives for Success
- Listens Actively
- Builds Rapport

All three skill areas are important to executing his job, and Lee's manager will be in a position to provide him feedback within his early weeks of training.

Lee's Development Objectives

To help Lee understand what's expected of him and to give him the direction and incentive he needs to improve in these areas without overwhelming him, he and his manager develop the objectives shown in Table 8-1.

It's important for both the manager and employee to commit to the plan and agree these are the most important goals.

To work through the tasks of developing and reviewing performance reviews as well as tackling difficult workplace issues, it helps to have good coaching skills. The ability to coach effectively can take many years of training and practice, but here some of the essentials.

Objective 1: Professional Development
Become thoroughly familiar with company products and services. Review sales training briefs, complete online assessments to demonstrate knowledge, and review questions with manager until briefing is complete. Demonstrate knowledge of new products by accompanying manager on sales calls for client introductions and new-product briefings. Participate in regional sales presentations for new-product introductions using prepared script and sales support for Q&A.

Objective 2: Performance
Listen actively. Practice summarizing key points during client presentations and looking for cues from clients to determine whether further explanation is necessary before moving on to the next subject. Allow time for discussion and applications of information to client-specific circumstances. Role-play with manager and/or peer to develop presentations that allow for discussion and client interaction. Ask manager for feedback following presentations.

Objective 3: Project Goals
Create sales goals with revenue projections for three months. Work with manager to develop weekly task sheet to determine where and how to divide time to close existing sales and develop new opportunities.

SIGNATURES AND APPROVALS	
Employee Signature	Date
Manager Signature	Date
VP/Dept. Head Signature	Date
HR Director Signature	Date

Table 8-1. Lee's Development Objectives

THE COACHING APPROACH TO DEVELOPMENT

Coaching is the process of developing employees by providing them the opportunity to grow and achieve optimal performance by receiving feedback, counseling, and mentoring. A coaching method that encourages participation in decision making will help your salespeople take ownership for the goals set. When employees expect feedback in a consistent and constructive way, you will have greater opportunity to influence the growth and development in an ongoing manner. Rather than relying solely on a review schedule, you will be in a better position to support your employees along the way to meeting their goals.

COMMUNICATION STYLES

One of the chief advantages for managers who have assessment data for their employees is understanding each employee's preferred communication style. By reviewing output from an assessment, you can adapt your communication style to each employee.

Take time to know your employees' preferred styles and try to accommodate them to the greatest extent possible as they will hear what you are saying more clearly and more easily.

There are seven steps that, when followed, will create a positive environment for providing feedback. Done in the right way, coaching is perceived as a roadmap for success and as a benefit. Done incorrectly and employees may feel berated, unappreciated, even punished. It's particularly important when creating a development plan to build a positive environment and gain buy-in to establish meaningful goals.

Step 1: Build a Relationship of Mutual Trust

The foundation of any coaching relationship is rooted in the manager's day-to-day relationship with the employee. Without some degree of trust, conducting an effective coaching meeting is impossible.

Step 2: Open the Meeting

In opening a coaching meeting, it's important for the manager to clarify, in a nonevaluative, nonaccusatory way, the specific reason the meeting was arranged. The key to accomplish this step for the manager is to restate the meeting purpose.

In restating the purpose, the manager briefly refers, in a friendly, nonjudgmental manner, to the specific reason for the meeting when the appointment was scheduled.

Step 3: Get Agreement

Probably the most critical step in the coaching meeting process is getting the employee to agree verbally that a performance issue exists. Overlooking or avoiding the performance issue because you assume the employee understands its significance is a typical mistake of managers. To persuade an employee a performance issue exists, a manager must be able to define the nature of the issue and get the employee to recognize the consequences of not changing his or her behavior. To do this you must specify the behavior and clarify the consequences.

The skill of specifying the behavior consists of three parts.

1. Cites specific examples of the performance issue
2. Clarifies his or her performance expectations in the situation
3. Asks the employee for agreement on the issue

The skill of clarifying consequences consists of two parts. The manager:

1. Probes to get the employee to articulate his or her understanding of the consequences associated with the performance issue
2. Asks the employee for agreement on the issue

Once the employee agrees that there is a performance issue that needs improvement or correction, the next step is to explore ways the issue can be improved or corrected.

Step 4: Explore Alternatives

The manager should explore by encouraging the employee to identify alternative solutions and should avoid jumping in to furnish his or her own alternatives, unless the employee is unable to think of any. The manager must also push for specific alternatives and not generalizations. The manager's goal in accomplishing this step is not to choose an alternative, which is the next step, but only to maximize the number of alternatives available for the employee to consider and to discuss their advantages and disadvantages.

This requires the skill of reacting and expanding. You want to:

◆ Acknowledge the employee's improvement suggestion

- Discuss the benefits and drawbacks of the suggestion
- Ask the employee for additional suggestions
- Offer suggestions he or she has not thought of
- Ask the employee to explain how to resolve the issue under discussion

After a sufficient number of alternatives have been discussed, the next step is to get the employee to commit to implementing the alternative(s) to best improve his or her performance situation.

Step 5: Get a Commitment to Act

The role of the manager is that of facilitator, helping the employee to choose an alternative. The manager shouldn't make the choice for the employee. To accomplish this step, the manager must be sure to get a verbal commitment from the employee regarding what action will be taken and when it will be taken.

This requires the skill of probe and support. The manager:

- Probes to encourage the employee to verbalize clearly the alternative(s) he or she intends to pursue, as well as when he or she plans to begin
- Supports the employee's choice of an alternative and offers praise

Step 6: Handle Excuses

Employee excuses may occur at any point during the coaching meeting. The key skills necessary to accomplish this step are to rephrase the point and respond empathically.

Rephrase the point by taking a comment or statement that was perceived by the employee to be blaming or accusatory and recasting it into one that encourages the employee to examine his or her behavior.

Respond empathically to show support for the employee's situation and communicate an understanding of both the content and feeling of the employee's comment.

Step 7: Provide Feedback

Effective coaches understand the value and importance of giving continual performance feedback to their people ... both positive and corrective. Author Ken Blanchard in *The One Minute Manager* (William Morrow, 1982) says that 80 percent of performance problems could have been solved if managers gave feedback more—regular performance feedback is the "breakfast of champions."

There are a few critical things to remember when giving feedback to others. Feedback should:

- Be timely. It should occur as soon as practical after the interaction, completion of the deliverable, or observation is made.
- Be specific. Statements like "You did a great job" or "You didn't take care of the clients' concerns very well" are too vague and don't give enough insight into the behavior you would like to see repeated or changed.
- Focus on the "what," not the "why." Avoid making the feedback seem as if it was a judgment. Begin with "I have observed ... " or "I have seen ... " and then refer to the behavior. Focus on behavior and not the person. Describe what you heard and saw and how those behaviors impact the team, client, etc.

Use a sincere tone of voice. Avoid a tone that exhibits anger, frustration, disappointment, or sarcasm.

Positive feedback strengthens performance. People will naturally go the extra mile when they feel recognized and appreciated. When corrective feedback is handled well, people will also experience the positive effects and performance is strengthened. When handled poorly, it will be a significant source of friction and conflict.

WHY ESTABLISH A MENTORING PROGRAM?

One of the most economical and rewarding ways to support your upwardly mobile star performers is through a mentoring program. Most companies have informal mentoring programs as a way to transfer knowledge and skills to others within the organization. Consider creating a more formal mentoring program. Your salespeople will view a mentoring relationship as a benefit and as something they can rely on to help further their careers. There's a process for structuring an effective mentoring program so that the results can be measured.

As with any program or initiative you begin, careful planning will increase the chances for a successful outcome. Following are recommended steps when establishing a mentoring program:

Step 1: Establish Objectives for the Program

What do you want to get out of the mentoring program? Here are some of the possibilities:

- Provide employee orientation
- Train new employees
- Teach technical skills
- Teach leadership skills

Step 2: Identify Mentees and Mentors

Matching prospective mentors and mentees can take on many shapes, depending on the objective.

Step 3: Establish Rules of Engagement

Before starting, determine how long the mentoring relationship will last. You can always elect to curtail or extend the relationship.

How often and for how long will you meet? Help those involved understand their time commitments and also gauge what level of support to expect.

Step 4: Assess Outputs

Assess the product and outcome of the mentoring relationship. Capture a review of what was accomplished during the period of engagement.

Step 5: Review Program

Create a questionnaire so those involved can report where a program is successful and where it can be improved. Did you accomplish what you set out to do?

Creating a positive environment for providing feedback will go a long way toward helping your salespeople feel appreciated. Having direction means they will keep moving forward in a way that's beneficial to employee and organization. You will also have a more open style of communication within the organization that will promote honesty. Problems will be uncovered and resolved more quickly. You will have a better educated sales force.

CREATING A PERFORMANCE APPRAISAL

When you've been using a coaching model to give employees feedback and set performance goals throughout the year, you will enter an annual or semiannual performance appraisal review meeting prepared with a thorough understanding of accomplishments, areas for continued improvement, and a path of advancement. The annual performance appraisal is a formal way to record for the larger company or organization what an individual has accomplished within the given period. Often the outcome is tied to salary and advancement, so creating a thorough appraisal is important for that reason, as well.

A list of daily tasks and responsibilities necessary to execute the job, as well as the competencies required to master the job, will serve as the basis for one part of the performance appraisal. The competencies you use should be detailed and specific to the employee position. They are often also targeted for the specific job title. Someone operating in an entry-level position will have different responsibilities than someone at a senior level.

Sometimes the roles and responsibilities within an organization can change, whether it's in reaction to a changing external business climate, company growth, or some other company evolution within the company. When you maintain a hiring-ready organization and one that encourages routine employee review and feedback, you'll revisit the specific job competencies often enough to ensure they are up-to-date and accurate.

This type of performance appraisal provides opportunities for your sales professionals to rate themselves and then compare your evaluation against theirs.

To provide an appraisal based on the competencies developed for a job, use a rating scale as well as comments that explain the ratings. Providing an evaluation with both perspectives will yield a more useful result. Only using words to describe performance can be misleading and misinterpreted. Employees can wrongly interpret the meaning. Some will be blind to their weaknesses, and others will judge themselves too harshly. Conversely some will minimize their successes, and others will overvalue them.

Every rating must be accompanied by sufficient descriptions and examples in the comments section to explain and justify the rank. These comments should point to how successful performance leads to on-the-job success. The comments section should also include specific goals for growth or ways to improve. Everyone is familiar with rating scales, and having clear, consistent descriptions makes ratings easy to interpret.

The manager reviews the competencies with the individual and discusses each competency rating and how well the individual is performing. The performance appraisal creates a way to review goals and continually set new challenges that will pave the way for success.

During the months leading up to his annual performance appraisal, Lee and his manager worked on Lee's ability to listen actively, one of the competencies identified on the hiring assessment as critical for his responsibilities in sales. For the annual review here is an example of how his manager rated his progress for the competency: *listens actively*. This is also a good example of a performance review template.

Sales Employee Performance Appraisal

Table 8-2 shows an example of a performance appraisal and the steps for completing one, and Table 8-3 presents a sample rating and performance comments.

Let's look at what a complete development assessment can show you and how you can use your findings for ongoing employee development.

Employee Name: Lee Washington   **Dept:** Sales

Employee Job Title: Outside Sales Representative

Manager: Eva Rios

Period: June 2009 to June 2010

X Annual   __ Semiannual   __ Other

Date of Completed Review: June 30, 2011

DEFINITION OF RATINGS

Exceptional (5): Exceeds all relevant performance standards.

Exceeds Expectations (4): Consistently meets and sometimes exceeds relevant performance standards.

Meets Expectations (3): Meets all relevant performance standards.

Below Expectations (2): Sometimes meets the performance standards. Seldom exceeds and falls short of desired results.

Needs Improvement (1): Consistently falls short of performance standards.

Describe the employee's contributions and professional strengths or areas needing development in each of the performance categories below. Illustrate specific, detailed examples of accomplishments and job-related behavior since the last review (or if hired this year, since the employee's date of hire). Rate each category according to the scale. Do not factor in a score for areas marked N/A ("not applicable"). Ratings must support and be substantiated by narrative comments. Continue comments on a separate sheet if needed. Send to HR for review prior to finalizing. Then return a fully signed and approved original to HR.

Table 8-2. Lee's Performance Appraisal

Listens Actively	N/A	1	2	3	4	5
1. Shows interest in hearing a wide variety of opinions.				X		
2. Takes time to engage others in dialogue.				X		
3. Skillfully incorporates feedback and input into conversation to understand people's behaviors and intentions.					X	
4. Summarizes key points during conversation to affirm understanding and build dialogue.				X		
5. Removes distractions from face-to-face communication.					X	
6. Asks relevant open-ended questions to build understanding.				X		

Average: 3.5

Comments: This is an area that Lee is aware he needs to continue working on to overcome his tendency to push on during conversations promoting his viewpoint without putting in enough effort to determine others' views. When he does provide an opportunity for feedback and listens, he does a good job of reflecting back others' input. He will improve by continuing to role-play as well as consciously preparing and asking open-ended questions to build dialogue.

Significant Achievements

Overall Average Score

Exceptional	Exceeds Expectations	Meets Expectations	Below Expectations	Needs Improvement

Table 8-3. Sample Rating and Performance Comments

CASE STUDY: EMPLOYEE DEVELOPMENT

Meet Jessica Michaels. Jessica is 34 and was recently hired as a sales account manager by a small company that customizes and resells SAP software solutions. She has just completed her sales training. The software she sells is complex, which requires a long sales cycle and draws upon her analytical skills to help customers apply the software solutions to solve their problems. Jessica's position requires technical competence to ensure clear communications between customers and sales support and to ensure specific client needs are addressed in a timely manner. Jessica excels as a salesperson, and customers find it easy to trust her because she is innovative and demonstrates technical and analytical competence.

Jessica's manager, Rob Hanson, is the director of sales. He has eight direct reports, each of whom is an account manager with several large accounts. He recognizes Jessica's strengths as a competent sales professional, yet he has been struggling with how to help her take her sales performance to the next level. His success is measured in part by staff improvement, and he knows that developing her sales skills will also help the company's bottom line. He values her technical and analytical abilities, which are an outstanding asset in this field, and he would like to see Jessica excel even further.

Rob sees that Jessica is goal focused and driven to succeed. Often when she focuses on a problem in the sales situation, however, she can become overly immersed in the data and lose track of time, continuing to work and rework a problem. Under stress, she can become overly critical and abrasive to those around her, in particular sales support, so people internally are reluctant to work with her. Rob has even had occasional feedback from customers, who say they are impressed with her innovation and problem-solving skills, but *also* say she can rub them the wrong way, especially when they question her analyses and prolong a buy decision.

Recently, her company implemented a companywide

employee assessment program to give managers the information they need to develop their employees. Jessica completed an assessment of her behaviors (DISC), core values, competencies, and thinking-style preferences.

Her manager has just received Jessica's assessment report results. He is impressed by how clearly the report reflects what he already knows about Jessica and is pleased with the advice the report provides for helping her develop. After he has reviewed the full report, he turns to the summary to help him focus on how he can use the information to communicate with Jessica. Let's walk through the process Rob uses to uncover Jessica's areas for improvement.

Reviewing the DISC Behavior Profile

In the results summary, the first section Rob looks at is Jessica's DISC profile. This is a summary of her behavioral tendencies and the way she approaches various work situations.

Figure 8-1 is Jessica's behavioral profile graph, which shows her scores on each of the four behavioral styles. The interpretations detailed in Table 8-4 (page 118) are grounded in these scores. The following sections include information based on primary behavioral styles, including potential strengths, weaknesses, and motivations.

Jessica scores high in D, which, as the category suggests, means she is driven to achieve results. Other factors contribute to her behavior, and predictably, the report highlights the strengths that help her sell complex solutions in a technical environment. Her high C scores indicate that she is fact and data driven and is oriented toward concepts, projections, and probabilities; has high concern for quality and accuracy; has considerable planning ability; and finds new and innovative ways to achieve results.

Potential limitations include a propensity toward bluntness, perfectionism, and overly controlling behavior. She can also appear cool and aloof while being overly critical of others, who find it difficult or impossible to live up to her expectations and

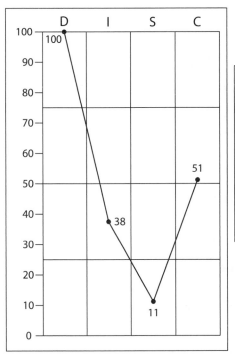

Figure 8-1. Jessica's behavior profile scores

standards. She is someone who can get bogged down in the data and be exceedingly cautious when making big decisions. Rob notes this has been an area of concern in past performance reviews.

COMPETENCY PROFILE SUMMARY

So far the results are consistent with other past reports and observations. The next area in the summary Rob reviews is the competency profile summary. This section highlights the top five competencies. Rob recalls that the competencies have been determined with questions that show how Jessica has responded to situations in the past. These are skills she uses in her work environment.

Strengths
◆ May be seen as being forceful, analytical, creative, and driving
◆ Tends to be fact and data driven, and oriented toward concepts, projections, and probabilities
◆ Tenaciously gathers and reviews facts looking for the right answer
◆ Considers all possible solutions before making a decision
◆ Has a high concern for quality and accuracy
◆ Demonstrates considerable planning ability
◆ Is decisive on daily matters
◆ Finds new and innovative ways to achieve results
◆ Drives change within the organization
◆ Is focused on tangible outcomes
◆ Maintains high standards for self and others
Potential Overextensions and Limitations
◆ May be seen as intense, blunt, aggressive, cool, or aloof
◆ May not always convey her creative ideas in a simple, understandable way
◆ Has a tendency toward perfectionism that can result in others finding it difficult or impossible to live up to her standards or expectations
◆ Becomes easily bored with routine
◆ Can be seen as overly controlling
◆ Is overly critical and demanding of others
◆ Is exceedingly cautious when making big decisions

Table 8-4. Jessica's behavioral strengths and possible limitations

Jessica's Competency Profile Summary

Table 8-5 presents the profile summary for Jessica's competency results, and Table 8-6 (page 120) outlines her strengths and potential areas for development.

Rob isn't surprised that the relationship skills fall into an area for potential development, and yet, looking at her competency profile strengths, he sees how she uses persuasion, articulate communication, and buy-in to help close sales, perhaps overcoming the need for relationship building and the personal touch. Her top five competencies also show how she delivers compelling presentations and strives for success.

Her bottom five competencies show important sales skills

Top Five Competencies
◆ Persuades and Influences
◆ Communicates Articulately
◆ Gains Buy-In
◆ Delivers Compelling Presentations
◆ Strives for Success
Bottom Five Competencies
◆ Displays Emotions Effectively
◆ Demonstrates Flexibility/Resilience
◆ Builds Rapport
◆ Establishes Credibility
◆ Listens Actively

Table 8-5. Jessica's profile summary

that can be improved: Displays Emotions Effectively, Demonstrates Flexibility/Resilience, Builds Rapport, Establishes Credibility, and Listens Actively.

CORE VALUES AND MOTIVATION PROFILE

When Rob looks at the summary for Jessica's core values and motivation, he smiles and sees where she gets her tenacity and motivation to succeed in this challenging software sales environment. She obviously loves the challenge of selling sophisticated software solutions to people who respect her competence and innovation.

Jessica's Values and Motivation Profile

The results in Figure 8-2 show Jessica's top three core values, and Table 8-7 describes what will motivate her.

Jessica enjoys work that allows her to take calculated risks and compete with others, and she will likely be motivated by recognition and her ability to influence others. Her motivation for achieving challenging goals, along with her willingness to put forth her innovative but carefully thought-out strategies in an environment where she can influence others, will contribute to a successful sales situation. Gaining a self-awareness of her

This individual possesses strengths in the following areas:

◆ *Persuades and Influences:* Is effective at persuading others to change their mind or alter behavior. Presents compelling rationale and options that focus on advantages.

◆ *Communicates Articulately:* Demonstrates an ability to speak clearly and concisely and shows skill in using expressiveness to convey important points in verbal communications.

◆ *Gains Buy-In:* Looks for alternatives to find win-win solutions and then negotiates deliverables and schedules.

◆ *Delivers Compelling Presentations:* Presents information with enthusiasm and expressiveness and adapts her presentation style to suit different audiences.

◆ *Strives for Success:* Is driven to achieve and eagerly accepts challenging assignments. Strives to deliver excellence.

Potential development areas:

◆ *Displays Emotions Effectively:* At times emotions may be too easy to read. May show frustration or impatience too easily.

◆ *Demonstrates Flexibility/Resilience:* May tend to stick to how things have been done in the past and be slow to adapt to change. May get easily discouraged when things don't go according to plan.

◆ *Builds Rapport:* Makes some effort to get to know and understand others, but may find it challenging to establish quick rapport with some individuals.

◆ *Establishes Credibility:* Presents information positively, but openly discusses negatives. Does not embellish the facts to sell her ideas, but may paint a more optimistic picture to gain others' support and business. Is unlikely to hide intentions, but may not proactively offer underlying motivations.

◆ *Listens Actively:* May need to ask more open-ended questions, listen more intently, and be more sensitized to the nonverbal cues during conversations.

Table 8-6. Jessica's strengths and potential areas for development

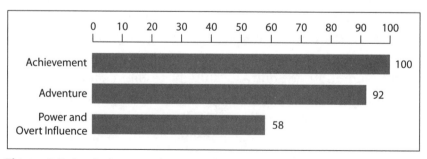

Figure 8-2. Jessica's core values scores

> **The top three values in this individual's report indicate the following:**
> ◆ She will be motivated by achieving challenging goals. (High Achievement)
> ◆ She will enjoy work that allows her to take calculated risks and compete with others. (High Adventure)
> ◆ She will be motivated by recognition, authority, and her ability to influence others. (High Power and Overt Influence)

Table 8-7. Jessica's top three core values

value system is a vital first step in self-development, as it allows her to reflect on what work is most rewarding. This plays an important part in developing a career path.

THINKING-STYLE PROFILE

The last summary Rob reviews is Jessica's thinking-style profile. This shows how she analyzes problems, evaluates information, and forms opinions based on patterns and preferences for thinking about, remembering, and using information.

Jessica's Thinking-Style Profile

As Figure 8-3 shows, Jessica scores highest in the innovative thinking style, indicating she will focus on new ideas, solutions, and opportunities when making decisions.

She also scores high in analytical thinking, so in many situations she will also collect data that will help her to consider the financial environment and leverage profitability when making decisions. Her results for strategic thinking show she will be

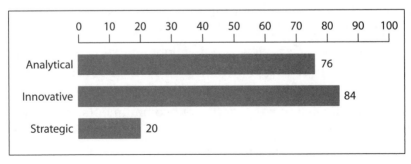

Figure 8-3. Jessica's thinking styles

less likely to focus on the long-term implications of her decisions. Table 8-8 highlights the results from Figure 8-3.

> ◆ Innovative thinking is greater than or equal to 84 percent of that of others in sales in her industry.
> ◆ Analytical thinking is greater than or equal to 76 percent of that of others in sales in her industry.
> ◆ Strategic thinking is greater than or equal to 20 percent of that of others in sales in her industry.

Table 8-8. Summary of Jessica's thinking-style results

JESSICA'S DEVELOPMENT PLAN

Jessica receives an assessment report that shows her results in detail and explains what her areas of strength are and where she has potential overextensions or limitations. After each profile (behavior, competencies, core values and motivation, and thinking styles), the report asks Jessica to reflect and report her observations. She should include comments surprised her, how her strengths help her in the workplace, what she sees that might be limiting, and then what specific actions or challenges she will take to change or adapt. Jessica meets with an internal coach who reviews the results with her. As part of her review and coaching session, Jessica completes the interactive reflection portions of the assessment report, which creates her development plan. Her development plan is then incorporated into the assessment report results.

Rob meets with Jessica to review the results. As they go through the full assessment report, Rob listens as Jessica notes how she responded to the interactive questions throughout.

Rob and Jessica review the development suggestions in the report for each of the profile areas and then review Jessica's development plan. When they have completed the review, they create specific action steps with time commitments, providing a clear plan of action that specifies how Jessica can use her strengths and that will help her work on areas of limitation or overextension. Here is a summary of Jessica's development plan.

Jessica's Development Plan Summary

Employee Name: Jessica Michaels

Organization: Sales

Date: 12/18/11

List the Behavioral Strengths That the Employee Identified:
- Has a high concern for quality and detail
- Is results oriented
- Is competitive and driven to achieve
- Makes careful decisions
- Maintains high standards for herself
- Has the ability to persuade and influence others
- Is successful at gaining buy-in and building long-term customer relationships
- Is a good listener

List the Behavioral Blind Spots That the Employee Identified:
- Can have a tendency to overanalyze
- Can overwhelm her customer with presentations that are too detailed
- Can spend excessive time researching a lead which can waste time
- Has difficulty delegating tasks to others

What Areas Would the Employee Like to Focus On?
- Delegating. Learning to let go and delegate more to her sales support
- Prospecting. Avoiding the tendency to spend excessive time researching
- Presentations. Stopping the tendency to present too much detail

What Action Steps Will the Employee Take to Improve in These Areas?
What does Jessica need to start, stop, or continue doing to improve? Jessica sets high standards for herself and is very detail oriented. She admits this can be a strength and a weakness, depending on the situation. She plans to focus on the following areas:
- Continue to research her leads but avoid the tendency to spend too much time gathering information. It will be valuable for Jes-

sica to set specific parameters for herself on the key information she will gather on a prospect before making the initial call and then stop researching.

♦ Learn to streamline her presentations, as she can present too much detail, which can be confusing or overwhelming to some customers.

What Top Competencies Has the Employee Committed to Work On?

Demonstrates Flexibility/Resilience:

♦ Jessica admits that while she likes variety in her job, having structure and consistency is important to her. She reviewed her lower score in demonstrating flexibility/resilience and the impact this may have for her in the workplace along with areas that may be important to focus on. She intends to work on:
  - Becoming more comfortable with changes even when she doesn't have all the detail.
  - Learning to let go and take support from others and delegate more tasks to her sales support. Take time to show others how she likes things done. She can always make edits and revisions later.

Displays Emotions Effectively:

♦ Jessica plans to pay closer attention to her ability to mask emotions, especially when under pressure. Asking for feedback from those she trusts and interacts with daily may also help her to become more aware of how her display of emotion may impact her and others.

What Jessica's Manager Learned

The assessment report shows that Jessica scored very high in the behavioral assessment in the Driving and Contemplating categories, revealing that she is task focused and tends to move quickly. Because she is impatient, Rob knows that to keep her moving forward, he needs to be very direct in his communication, providing ongoing feedback. One way he can support her is to help her remove obstacles and roadblocks and to get back to her quickly when he communicates. Because she moves so quickly, oftentimes she won't think something through. So another important way he can support her is by helping her think through her decisions.

Because she is so highly innovative, she'll see the big ideas. What Rob needs to do is help her think through the process of how things connect. Otherwise, Jessica will be off thinking about these big ideas and will get frustrated because she's not able to execute them.

In her core values he sees that she is goal focused because of the high score in the achievement category. She likes a little bit of adventure, and she's motivated by power and overt influence. She's a risk taker and goal focused. So something else Rob will do to help Jessica is to make sure that she has specific goals, not only in achieving revenue, but in targeting new selling categories and new industries or in taking a new idea and pitching it. Jessica needs to feel that she is innovating, groundbreaking, a change agent, and opening up uncharted territory. Rob knows it's in both their interests to support her in those efforts while still helping her think through how to get something done from start to finish.

Looking at her competencies, Rob knows that she tends to be emotional and inflexible. Rob needs to continue to work with her to help her with her emotions and show her that expressing them so overtly doesn't help her get what she wants in moving her projects forward. She needs to build connections with people, and it's not just about checking it off her list and getting the task done. She needs to take the time to build rapport over time and not just show that she is competent. People know she is competent, but she tends to think that her competence will earn that rapport along with credibility. Rob needs to show her that she'll get better results if she holds back on her emotional responses. Also, she doesn't always recognize that her lack of flexibility gets in her way. Rob will help her create good habits so that she becomes a better listener. Her mind is racing, and she's moving so quickly that often she doesn't take time to really listen to what a customer is communicating.

What a wealth of information to prepare Rob for helping Jessica take her sales career to the next level!

Not all assessments are the same or contain all the components described in this case study. However, as you can see, looking at a diverse set of data gathered either during the hiring process or from an existing employee provides a wealth of insight that will support and strengthen even your top performers. Recognizing their strengths and offering support to help them achieve even more will go a long way toward retaining them longer.

MOVING FORWARD

Using development plans for your individual salespeople sets expectations for performance reviews, but more important, provides opportunities for ongoing feedback, coaching, and training, so that growth and improvement are an ongoing process. You can also use assessments to similarly analyze your entire sales team. You can use the results as part of the process for creating your benchmark. In the next chapter, a case study examines a sales team analysis, strengths and weaknesses of this team, and how using data provides guidance for developing the current team members.

Chapter

9 Finding and Fixing the Gaps in Your Sales Team

As you travel down life's highway … whatever be your goal, you
cannot sell a doughnut without acknowledging the hole.

—Harold J. Shayler

ACCULECT IS A SMALL ELECTRONICS TECHNOLOGY COMPANY. VICE PRESIDENT OF Sales Jack LaFleur's sales team will be expanding to cover an increase in the number of new products and a rapidly growing business. Jack, a seasoned senior executive, inherited this team that he is now overseeing. Before expanding the department, he wants to update the job description and job benchmark so he has a clear view of what soft skills and problem-solving skills are required for the job. He also wants to have a complete view of these skills for his current team.

By using assessments that measure competencies and behaviors, core values and motivators, and critical thinking skills, he will have a better understanding of what skill gaps exist in the team. He can use that information in addition to the benchmark for hiring new team members that fit the job and the current team best. At the same time he will have information to help develop the current team members and address areas of weakness.

First we'll look at the attributes and assessment results for the team as a whole. Then we'll focus on an individual team member's attributes and assessment results and each team member's development plans.

The AccuLect Company sales team's data showed the following strengths:

- A strong focus on building customer relationships
- Strong communication skills
- Ability to adapt and work effectively with diverse situations and groups
- Active in supporting and promoting the organization
- Ability to handle conflict effectively

The lower-scoring areas for the AccuLect Company sales team indicated that the team:

- Is weaker in active listening—may make decisions before listening to and clarifying information
- May wait for approval before taking action and may not adequately anticipate obstacles
- Is less competitive; not strongly motivated by winning or surpassing the performance of others
- May lack sufficient negotiation skills and may have difficulty reaching an appropriate compromise during a negotiation
- Is strongly motivated by developing relationships and servicing customers versus driving results, and at times may settle for less if there are too many obstacles

Team Values Observations

The AccuLect Company sales team is motivated by:

- Engaging in work that involves service to others
- Developing relationships
- Being creative and trying new approaches
- Developing new ideas and solutions

Comparison to Job Profile

Table 9-1 shows the potential of AccuLect's sales team in comparison with the job requirements identified in the Job Profile Report. As you can see, all fall into the same area of moderate potential. The goal for any hiring manager is to have as many team members as possible in the high potential and moderate/high potential categories. When you reach that goal, you'll know that you have the right people in the job.

High Potentials
Moderate/High Potentials
Moderate Potentials
Brent Taft
Larry Raye
Will Franklin
Frank Fontana
Annette Sullivan
Moderate/Low Potentials
Low Potentials

Table 9-1. AccuLect team comparison with job profile

Team Behavioral Results

Figure 9-1 maps the behaviorial preferences (team quadrant) for the five team members. The sales manager, Jack, can use this graph to view his high and low performers and to serve as a guide to lead and motivate each team member.

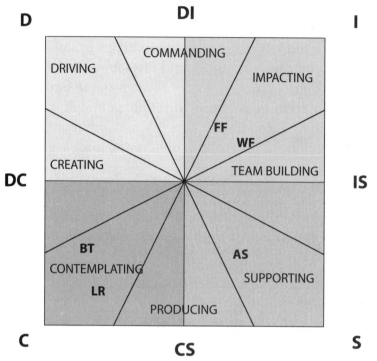

Figure 9-1. AccuLect company sales team quadrant

The graph plots the initials of the team members in their corresponding dominant segments. Here is what the analysis says about the team members and their behavioral tendencies.

The AccuLect Company Sales Team Behavioral Observations

- (BT) Brent Taft is focused on detail and process. He will take a more cautious approach to making decisions and achieving results.
- (LR) Larry Raye is thorough and will take a methodical approach to decision making. He is good at creating systems, procedures, and processes.
- (FF) Frank Fontana is focused on building rapport and influencing and motivating others.
- (WF) Will Franklin is collaborative and is a supportive team player focused on creating harmony and building consensus.

THE PERFECT HIRE

- ◆ (AS) Annette Sullivan is methodical and is focused on servicing and supporting others.

This profile report shows the diversity of behavioral preferences within the group.

After reviewing the group results for potential and studying the behavioral team graph, Jack LaFleur looks at the individual reports and the development plans for each person. Here is an example of a complete report to show the different perspectives a detailed individual development profile can provide.

BRENT TAFT'S ASSESSMENT RESULTS

Following are the results of Brent Taft's assessment, including a broad range of charts and graphs that depict where his strengths and weaknesses lie in relation to the Job Profile Report. Figure 9-2 provides summary charts for each of the assessment areas (competencies, core values, behaviors, and thinking styles) followed by a summary explaining each area of the results.

The profile summary captures Brent's assessment results in a snapshot. First the summary identifies the five competencies in the Job Profile Report in which Brent scored highest and then lists the five competencies in which he scored lowest. Next it shows Brent's top three values. The two behavioral charts show his innate preferred style (Contemplating/Driving) and his expressed style (Contemplating), which is how he adapts his preferred style to his current environment. Last, they show Brent's preferred thinking style, or how he prefers to process information.

Table 9-2 shows Brent's scores in detail: how he rated compared with other successful salespeople for the top seven competencies required for the job, the three critical thinking skills, and the core values in rank order of importance to the job. Good reports will present the data in a number of ways, both visually and with clearly written descriptions for interpreting the data. Figure 9-3 provides Brent's results showing his scores for each of the job-required competencies, then the three areas

Top Five Competencies
◆ Displays Emotions Effectively
◆ Enjoys Winning
◆ Embodies Organizational Image
◆ Gains Buy-in
◆ Communicates Accurately

Bottom Five Competencies
◆ Builds Rapport
◆ Strives for Success
◆ Develops and Maintains Relationships
◆ Listens Actively
◆ Delivers Compelling Presentations

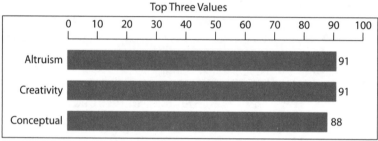

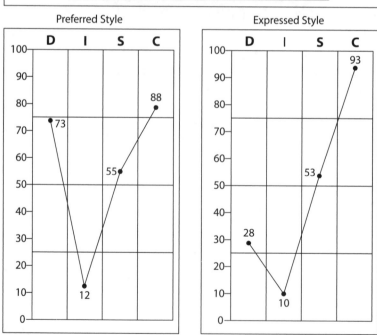

Figure 9-2. Brent Taft's profile summary

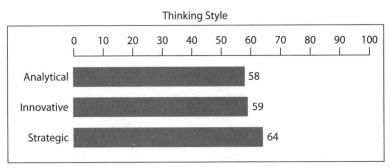

Figure 9-2. Brent Taft's profile summary (continued)

	High	Scores greater than 79
	Moderate	Scores between 40 and 79
	Low	Scores below 40

Overall Rank	Competency	Score
1	Seizes opportunities	56
2	Demonstrates flexibility/resilience	55
3	Builds customer loyalty	48
4	Gains buy-in	69
5	Maintains endurance	9
6	Communicates articulately	7
7	Develops and maintains relationships	19
Overall Rank	**Critical Thinking**	**Score**
1	Reasons logically	49
2	Reasons numerically	46
3	Reasons verbally	8
Overall Rank	**Values**	**Score**
1	Achievement	6
2	Power and overt influence	4
3	Adventure	92

Table 9-2. Brent Taft's assessment results summary

of critical thinking followed by a written interpretation.

Having the data is one thing; understanding it is another. So explaining the information comes next, starting with the top and bottom five competencies.

Brent Taft's Competency Observations
Top Five Competencies

- Expresses reactions and opinions with genuine emotion; emotions are not hidden but also not overblown. Handles intense interactions and emotionally charged situations effectively. (Displays Emotions Effectively)
- Likes to win and seeks to find a better way. Works hard to exceed and surpass the performance of others. (Enjoys Winning)
- Supports and actively promotes the organization. Positively reflects the organization's core values and addresses actions that don't align with those values. (Embodies Organizational Image)
- Explores alternatives and positions to reach outcomes that gain the support and acceptance of all parties. (Gains Buy-In)
- Speaks clearly and concisely; uses appropriate amount of expressiveness to convey important points. (Communicates Articulately)

Bottom Five Competencies

- May not establish rapport quickly with others and may make little effort to understand others or find common ground. (Low score for Builds Rapport)
- May not feel that attaining organizational goals is a source of internal satisfaction. May feel that the goals of the organization are overly optimistic or unrealistic and may settle for less if there are too many obstacles. (Low score for Strives for Success)
- May be more responsive vs. proactive in developing and maintaining relationships, contacting others only when

there is a specific business purpose. May not look to build relationships beyond his immediate sphere of influence. (Low score for Develops and Maintains Relationships)

◆ May only hear half the story before drawing conclusions. May not summarize key points to ensure understanding before moving on to new topics. (Low score for Listens Actively)

◆ May not present information with appropriate amount of enthusiasm or expressiveness; may not make adjustments to presentation style to suit different audiences. (Low score for Delivers Compelling Presentations)

Here is a brief description interpreting the other results shown on the chart:

◆ Competency scores: Four of the top seven competencies are a moderate fit, and three score as a low fit.

◆ Critical thinking scores: Two critical thinking areas score as a moderate fit, and one scores as a low fit.

◆ Core values scores: Achievement and Social score as a low fit. Altruism scores as a high fit.

The percentile scores given in Table 9-2 for the seven most important job competencies are displayed in Figure 9-3 as a bar graph. This view is easier for some to understand the data. It also provides the summary competency score of moderate, which shows Brent's overall potential.

Even more important than having the data and descriptions is knowing what to do with them. How can the information help improve performance, identify areas for growth, and increase the fit between the salesperson's competency and the job? After reviewing Brent's assessment results with his boss, Jack and Brent agreed on a development plan for Brent based on those results. .

For the rest of the four team members, Jack LaFleur

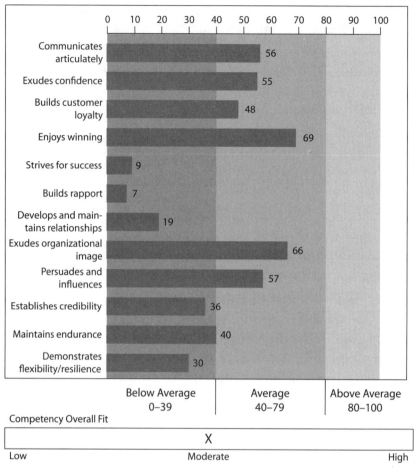

Figure 9-3. Brent Taft's competency

Development Plan Summary

Organization: The AccuLect Company

Employee Name: Brent Taft

Date: 3/30/11

List the behavioral strengths that the employee identified in his or her profile:
- ◆ Industry experience
- ◆ Logical and factual in his approach
- ◆ Highly organized

- Detail focused
- Supportive of customers
- High standards for quality

List the behavioral blind spots that the employee identified in his or her profile:
- Can be too much of a perfectionist at times
- May be seen as inflexible until he understands a new direction or change

What are the areas that the employee would like to focus on?
- Communicating/building rapport
- Time management/preparation; continue to look for ways to minimize time spent on preparation and on creating the process

What are the top competencies that the employee has committed to working on?

Demonstrates Flexibility/Resilience:
- Brent admits that he can be a perfectionist at times and can spend too much time on creating the process versus executing it. He recognizes that it will be beneficial to learn to establish boundaries for himself and determine when something is good enough and he can move on to the next priority.
- Brent manages through change best when he has adequate information and an understanding of the change. Without this understanding, he may come across as inflexible, and it can be hard to change his point of view. He wants to continue to get better at keeping an open mind until he has a full understanding.

Strives for Success, Seizes Opportunities:
- Brent has a long history with the company and is often called upon by customers and others to handle things beyond his main area of responsibility. He enjoys being a resource and helping others but finds this can cause him to get sidetracked from his own goals. He wants to get better at setting boundaries around the amount of time he spends on these types of side initiatives.

Builds Rapport:
Brent is typically very logical and straightforward in his approach. To enhance his ability to build rapport quickly with new customers, he would like to focus on the following:

- Avoid jumping right into business with new customers. Look for common ground and spend a moment or two making small talk.
- Make note of his customers' interests and other personal information they reveal and then bring them up in conversation.
- Ask others for feedback on the body language that he projects. Work on displaying more relaxed and open behaviors that can help to break the ice or put others at ease.

receives a similar report, including the graphs and detailed explanation along with the comprehensive development report. Rather than review each of the results for the other team members, let's look at the development reports, which summarize areas of achievement and areas for improvement.

LARRY RAYE'S DEVELOPMENT PLAN

Here is the development plan for Larry Raye based on the assessment results.

Development Plan Summary

Organization: The AccuLect Company

Employee Name: Larry Raye

Date: 4/5/11

List the behavioral strengths that the employee identified in his or her profile:
- Highly detail focused
- Very organized, thorough, and great with follow-through
- Customer service oriented
- High standards for quality
- Ability to multitask
- Collaborative and accommodating
- Strong presentation skills
- Ability to manage conflict situations and turn angry customers around

List the behavioral blind spots that the employee identified in his or her profile:

◆ Has a tendency to overanalyze and get bogged down in little details
◆ Can be too much of a perfectionist at times
◆ Can have a difficult time relaxing and pacing himself

What are the areas that the employee would like to focus on?

◆ Listening
◆ Decision making; avoiding the tendency to overanalyze
◆ Time management; overcoming his perfectionism so he is spending less time on lower-priority tasks

What action steps will the employee take to improve in these areas? (What does he or she need to start, stop, or continue doing or modify to improve in these areas?)

Larry recognizes that at times he can be too much of a perfectionist. Learning to discern which tasks and activities require his very detailed approach and where he can settle for good enough will be beneficial.

Larry is a worrier and has a tendency to overanalyze the little things that can slow him down. He wants to get better at letting go of the small things and the things he can't control. One key area for him is to gain perspective on the consequences of being wrong. It is likely that the consequences are far lower than he perceives.

Larry has a lot of experience in the job and is often called upon by others in the company as a resource. He has good insight into ways in which the company can improve its processes but admits that he typically tends to wait until he is called upon to share his ideas. He wants to get better at being proactive in sharing his ideas.

What are the top competencies that the employee has committed to working on?

Innovative Thinking Style:

◆ Larry scored lower in the innovative thinking style. His typical approach is to stick with what he knows has worked in the past vs. looking for new ideas and solutions. He is working on being more open minded and willing to look at new approaches. When working to solve problems, he may benefit by trying to view every problem from two or three different perspectives before making a final decision.

Listens Actively:

◆ Larry has an active mind. To improve his listening, he sees that he needs to slow down and avoid jumping ahead in his mind so he is stays actively engaged in the present conversation.

WILL FRANKLIN'S DEVELOPMENT PLAN

Here is the development plan for Will Franklin based on the assessment results.

Development Plan Summary

Organization: The AccuLect Company

Employee Name: Will Franklin

Date: 3/29/11

List the behavioral strengths that the employee identified in his or her profile:

◆ Cooperation and collaboration
◆ Easy rapport with others
◆ Very people oriented and supportive
◆ Strong focus on customer service
◆ Strong relationships with customers and others
◆ Competitive; likes to win
◆ Ability to manage emotions effectively

List the behavioral blind spots that the employee identified in his or her profile:

◆ Can trust too quickly
◆ At times may have a tendency to overservice
◆ Dislikes conflict; in an effort to avoid a confrontational situation, may not always speak up

What are the areas that the employee would like to focus on?

◆ Adapting his approach when working with analytical-style customers
◆ Qualifying; asking more questions to get validation before trusting
◆ Looking for more innovative solutions versus sticking with what has worked in the past

---

What action steps will the employee take to improve in these areas? (What does he or she need to start, stop, or continue doing or modify to improve in these areas?)

◆ Will recognizes that he can be too trusting and take what his customers say at face value. He knows he needs to continually work on asking additional questions before accepting what he hears to ensure he has validation to back up what he has heard.

What are the top competencies that the employee has committed to working on?

Seizes Opportunities:

◆ Will now has three sales centers that he will be working with, and so he recognizes that he will need to place a stronger emphasis on uncovering business opportunities to drive business (builders, developers, contractors, etc.) to these centers.

Establishes Credibility:

◆ Will relies on his strong people skills when he is working to influence others. We discussed the importance of ensuring he is presenting adequate facts and details when working with the more analytical customers to enhance his credibility with this style.

Innovative Thinking Style:

◆ Will scored lower in the innovative thinking style. His typical approach is to stick with what he knows has worked in the past vs. looking for new ideas and solutions. When working to solve problems, he may benefit by trying to view every problem from two or three perspectives before making a final decision. Seeking out others who tend to be more innovative to help him brainstorm ideas may be helpful.

FRANK FONTANA'S DEVELOPMENT PLAN

Here is the development plan for Frank Fontana based on the assessment results.

Development Plan Summary

Organization: The AccuLect Company

Employee Name: Frank Fontana

Date: 3/30/11

List the behavioral strengths that the employee identified in his or her profile:

- People focused
- Cooperative, supportive, and collaborative
- Optimistic
- Ease in developing rapport and relationships with customers
- Innovative, outside-of-the-box thinker
- Ability to control emotions to manage difficult customer situations
- Enjoyment of winning; focused on developing strategies to beat the competition

List the behavioral blind spots that the employee identified in his or her profile

- Can be too trusting
- Dislikes conflict; may internalize his thoughts and feelings to avoid conflict
- Can be too tolerant or indirect in holding others accountable
- Sensitive to criticism; can take it personally at first

What are the areas that the employee would like to focus on?

- Listening
- Adapting his approach to match his customer's behavioral-style tendencies
- Presentations

What action steps will the employee take to improve in these areas? (What does he or she need to start, stop, or continue doing or modify to improve in these areas?)

- A tendency to dislike conflict and be overly tolerant came out as a potential blind spot in Frank's profile. He recognizes he may not always be as direct with or willing to provide constructive feedback to others who don't deliver on commitments. This is an area he would like to focus on.

What are the top competencies that the employee has committed to working on?

Enjoys Winning, Maintains Strategic Business Perspective:

◆ Frank scored high in competencies related to understanding the competition in order to leverage the company's ability to capture market share. He sees this as a continued area for focus and development.

Gains Buy-In:

◆ To improve his ability to communicate effectively and gain customer buy-in, Frank may benefit from becoming more sensitized to the behavioral style of his customer. This will help him to ensure that he is interacting with and presenting to them by using an approach and the amount and type of information that meets their style needs.

◆ We discussed how he could use some of the communication methods and suggestions in his development assessment report to help him consider how to best adapt to working with different styles.

Listens Actively:

◆ Listening is an area Frank feels he can continue to improve in. We discussed the following:
  - Catch himself if he is jumping ahead or focusing on his response versus what is being said.
  - Take notes to remind himself of a point he wants to make so he can stay focused on the conversation.
  - Ask more questions or reflect back what he thinks he heard to be sure he has heard the details.

ANNETTE SULLIVAN'S DEVELOPMENT PLAN

Here is the development plan for Annette Sullivan based on the assessment results.

Development Plan Summary

Organization: The AccuLect Company

Employee Name: Annette Sullivan

Date: 3/31/11

List the behavioral strengths that the employee identified in his or her profile:
- Ease in building rapport
- Strong customer relationships
- Strong emphasis on customer service
- Collaborative and supportive
- Creative and innovative; works with her customers to find creative ways to move business forward
- Passion for training

List the behavioral blind spots that the employee identified in his or her profile:
- Dislikes confrontation
- Can be too indirect at times
- Can take criticism personally at times

What are the areas that the employee would like to focus on?
- Being more assertive
- Managing time better

What action steps will the employee take to improve in these areas? (What does he or she need to start, stop, or continue doing or modify to improve in these areas?)

Deals with Conflict:

Annette is a strong team player who is very supportive of others. Her dislike of conflict and confrontation can cause her to be overly tolerant or to give people too much slack at times. The following are areas that Annette wants to focus on:
- Being more direct and assertive
- Considering the situations where it will be important for her to speak up and express her thoughts and feelings
- Addressing issues and problems sooner

What are the top competencies that the employee has committed to working on?

Gains Buy-In:

Gains Buy-In was one of Annette's lower-scoring competencies. We discussed becoming more sensitized to the style of her customers to be sure she is using the appropriate approach and amount and type of information to meet their style needs. For example, when working with direct, assertive, aggressive customers:

- Be prepared with a shorter, "CliffsNotes" version of her presentation as they prefer a fast-paced, bottom-line approach.
- Enhance her ability to identify buying signals—avoid the tendency to tell the whole story before asking for the close.

When working with detail-oriented, analytical customers:

- Tone down the amount of enthusiasm and animation she uses.
- Slow down and provide more facts and a logical flow to the presentation.

Strives for Results:

- Annette finds she can underestimate the amount of time certain tasks or projects will take, which can impact her ability to prioritize her time well. While she gets it done, it is often at the expense of her own personal time. She wants to get better at first thinking a project or initiative through and setting realistic expectations for herself.

SUMMARY

The information provided in the sales team analysis will help Jack round out his team and the team performance by hiring new team members that complement their skills. The results confirm that Jack will need to look outside for a team leader and those with drive who will challenge and raise the bar for the other team members.

MOVING FORWARD

By using assessments with a sales team, you will be able to identify gaps, needs, or complementary skills that will help take your current team to a higher level of performance. Looking at overall strengths and areas for improvement, will help you give your team additional support. It will also provide guidance for hiring new team members.

Just as important as having results to help in making hiring decisions, there are specific areas you can assess to help your salespeople excel, provide a growth path, or use as part of a succession plan. Understanding what the results mean will give you greater insight into how to apply and use them. The next chapter looks in detail at the kinds of attributes you can measure that are most helpful for developing your salespeople.

Chapter

10 Using Data and Benchmarks to Develop and Manage Your Employees

Leadership: The art of getting someone else to do something you want done because he wants to do it.

—Dwight D. Eisenhower, U.S. President

A PRACTICAL TOOL FOR LEARNING ABOUT THE DIFFERENCES IN COMMUNICATION styles and for identifying the behavioral strengths and weaknesses of a sales team is behavioral profiling. This can also be used as a team-building tool to integrate new members into sales teams, and it can be used for sales teams themselves. Behavioral style reflects the way a person interacts with others in the workplace and the ways in which a person approaches his or her job. Each person has a preferred style of giving and receiving information. The lack of understanding of these styles often causes miscommunication, misconceptions, and even conflict. Discovering the differences and working with each person's boundaries greatly helps in smoothing the flow of communication and managing your sales force.

Through behavioral profiling, you can learn the communication dos and don'ts for working effectively with anyone, including staff members, peers, and bosses. You can learn the best way to motivate and coach each person on your staff. Salespeople who understand how to adapt their style to communicate more effectively with customers will be more successful developing rapport, communicating in e-mail, writing proposals, and making verbal presentations. Knowledge of their own style and how to interact with other styles is essential.

In the recruiting process, behavior profiling can be used to determine which job candidates are most likely to fit in well with your company's culture and with your team. Finally, by learning more about your own behavior style, you can identify tendencies that may be holding you back or strengths that you can build on to push toward success.

Using behavioral profiling, you can assess the strengths and weaknesses of your sales team and identify gaps that may exist.

HISTORY OF DISC

One of the most widely used behavioral profiling tools, and one that we frequently use with clients, is our own version of the DISC profile. It's based on William Moulton Marston's *Emotions of Normal People*, which he wrote in 1928. Although Marston was the major developer of the DISC language, the concept of categorizing how people behave into four categories dates back much earlier.

> ### Behavioral Profiling Dates Back to Hippocrates
>
> Hippocrates, in the second century BCE, described personality disorders or physical illnesses as the result of one of four humors being out of balance. The words evolving from what Hippocrates called these dominant temperaments are still in use today: *sanguine, phlegmatic, melancholic,* and *choleric.*

More recently, other theorists have also described predominant behavioral tendencies in four categories. Carl Jung, for example, used *sensing, intuitive, feeling,* and *thinking.* Marston, however, may have been the first to use the four-category model to describe behaviors of normal people. At first, his DISC assessment was mostly used by the U.S. Army for recruiting, but it's now used extensively by the general population. Several versions of the DISC profile are available on the market today, including online versions that are quick and easy to use.

The DISC language is based on observable behavior. The DISC model analyzes behavioral style, that is, a person's manner of doing things. It provides a way to assess the various ways people behave under certain circumstances, their motivators, their most natural attributes, their behavior in the work environment, and their preferred communication styles.

The DISC model is a development tool as well; it helps people learn how to communicate, interact, and manage their communications. While individuals cannot change their personalities, they can learn to change the way they behave to improve their communication and relationships with others, especially with those who have different behavioral styles. All styles can be more or less effective depending on how individuals use information about their style to modify their behavior to meet the needs of other people and the environment.

Behavioral profiling is valuable in determining the best ways in which to communicate with an individual—what not to say, what to say, and how to say it so the recipient listens. It's important to understand the behaviors of those you manage, and it's important for salespeople to understand behaviors and how they affect communication so they can interact more effectively with customers.

DETERMINE YOUR STYLE

To give you a better understanding of how behavioral profiling works, here's a short survey to help you identify some of the behavioral tendencies you may exhibit. Each of the four boxes in Table 10-1 contains 20 adjectives. Think how each of the adjectives describes you; then check all that apply to you in each section. Total the checks you've made in each box. The box with the highest total is usually the one that best describes you best. Although your scores may be close in more than one section, most people have personal styles that match just one or two, but rarely all four. The behavioral styles, as defined by the DISC model, are described in the section following the survey.

Box 1		Box 2	
❏ Ambitious	❏ Forceful	❏ Animated	❏ Life of the party
❏ Fast-paced	❏ Lots of drive	❏ Big-picture person	❏ Sociable
❏ Demanding	❏ Strong-willed	❏ Not detail-oriented	❏ Confident
❏ Controlling	❏ Take charge	❏ Energetic	❏ Sense of humor
❏ Courageous	❏ Independent	❏ Innovative	❏ Like variety
❏ Outcome-oriented	❏ Venturesome	❏ Persuasive	❏ Charming
❏ Opinionated	❏ Easily bored	❏ Spontaneous	❏ Curious
❏ Decisive	❏ Leader	❏ Outgoing	❏ Warm
❏ Take Risks	❏ Assertive	❏ Enthusiastic	❏ Impulsive
❏ Competitive	❏ Inquisitive	❏ Trusting	❏ Laugh easily
Box 3		**Box 4**	
❏ Consistent	❏ Loyal	❏ Intellectual	❏ Systematic
❏ Methodical	❏ Passive	❏ Goes by the rules	❏ Idealistic
❏ Predictable	❏ Steady	❏ Traditional	❏ Painstakingly accurate
❏ Empathic	❏ Understanding		
❏ Relaxed	❏ Patient	❏ Private	❏ Neat
❏ Peacemaker	❏ Easygoing	❏ Diplomatic	❏ Perfectionist
❏ Pleasant	❏ Reserved	❏ Deliberate	❏ Withhold self
❏ Dislikes conflict	❏ Systematic	❏ High standards	❏ Detail-oriented
❏ Careful	❏ Cooperative	❏ Consider all opinions	❏ Predictable
❏ Concern for others	❏ Objective	❏ Hesitant to act	❏ Thorough
		❏ Organized	❏ Orderly

Table 10-1. Quick behavior-type survey

THE DISC BEHAVIORAL STYLES

The traditional DISC acronym stands for Dominant, Influence, Steadiness, and Conscientiousness. We've updated the terminology to reflect terms that are less derogatory and value-laden and more contemporary. DISC: Driving, Impacting, Supporting, and Contemplating. These are the four core behaviors that all people can use to categorize their preferred behavioral styles. There are, by all means, many combinations of the four styles, and that is what makes us all unique.

Box 1: Driving (Dominant)

Individuals who show a high Driving style are those who tend to process quickly and are focused on tasks. These people tend to be results oriented, focus on challenge and power, and like to make decisions quickly with confidence. They are the team members who you know will get the job done.

Some descriptors of this style include *driving, demanding, aggressive, pioneering,* and *competitive.* Individuals with a high Driving style prefer to be evaluated on the results and not the process. They are goal driven and enjoy a personal challenge.

When you receive communication from someone who is high in Driving, it could appear short, undetailed, overpowering, intimidating, insensitive to feelings, or impatient. You may need to ask for additional information, as Driving types often communicate in short bursts.

Team members who are Driving oriented will be at their best when solving problems and driving for results. They are positive, powerful, and authoritative. Driving-oriented team members, however, will not be shy to overstep boundaries and use fear as a motivator. Further, they are known for their lack of listening skills and tact. They are often unhappy with routine work; they also overdelegate and underinstruct.

If you think you fall into the Driving category, you would help the communications process by improving your listening skills, being more patient, toning down directness, and asking more questions.

Here is a summary of common strengths and areas to bring awareness to those who exhibit high Driving characteristics.

General Strengths

- Ability to manage multiple priorities with ease
- Ability to react well in a fast-paced, changing environment
- Willingness to take risks
- Assertiveness; direct and straightforward communication style

- Decisiveness
- Results oriented
- Enterprising; seek new and innovative ways to achieve results

Sales Strengths

- Thrive on competition
- Give presentations that are typically energetic and results focused
- Are tenacious, not easily discouraged
- Create a sense of urgency in selling situations
- Aren't afraid to ask for the sale

General Blind Spots

- Can be too focused on task and less focused on people
- May come across as short, intimidating, or insensitive to feelings
- Can be blunt; directness can be interpreted as confrontational
- Uses a bottom-line approach that can cut people off
- May be seen as bossy or argumentative; can be impulsive, speak before thinking
- Are impatient, especially when others are slow to understand or commit
- Sometimes move too fast; tendency to take on too much at once
- Make changes without planning

Sales Blind Spots

- Show impatience with slow decision makers or processes that slow down their ability to get results
- Tend to dive right in and work without a plan
- May move too quickly and not listen carefully
- May jump to a conclusion too quickly or make promises for others to keep
- May push too hard or try to close too soon for some buyers
- Tend to avoid paperwork or be late in completing it

When you manage sales employees who exhibit high Driving characteristics, then you will want to be sure to understand their preferred work environment motivators and the following tips for managing them.

Work Environment Motivators

◆ Challenging assignments
◆ Freedom from tasks with excessive details
◆ Nonroutine tasks and activities; variety
◆ Freedom to achieve results in their own way
◆ Opportunity to try the untried; innovate
◆ Control over own destiny; authority to achieve results

Implications for Management

◆ Avoid micromanagement
◆ Understand their tendency to get bored easily; provide challenging assignments
◆ Help to remove obstacles hindering results
◆ Provide flexibility whenever possible; clearly define boundaries they cannot cross
◆ Provide opportunity for advancement
◆ Provide direct, timely feedback
◆ Compliment on results and achievement

Box 2: Impacting (Influence)

Individuals who show a high Impacting style are those who tend to process quickly and are focused on people. They are the team members who keep things exciting and keep everyone motivated. Recognition, relationships, and freedom from details will likely motivate them.

Team members who have a high Impacting style will need to be given time to socialize. Not afraid to have fun, they ask for feelings and opinions, and they often show their best work during brainstorming sessions.

Impacting people have a need to verbalize. They also lack attention to detail, appear superficial, have poor follow-through, and can appear manipulative. Impacting people most likely will talk around a subject until they are able to make their point. You may find yourself exercising a lot of patience with the Impacting behavioral style.

Impacting people are socially and verbally aggressive; they bring optimism and have good persuasion skills and a vision of the big picture. They are people oriented and team oriented. Individuals who exhibit Impacting are impulsive and unrealistic in appraising people, and they often cannot pay attention to detail and are frequently disorganized.

If you fall into the Impacting category, you can improve your communication with others by listening to the real needs of the person with whom you are speaking, being more organized, and being specific in direction and praise.

Here is a summary of common strengths and areas to bring awareness to those who exhibit high Impacting characteristics.

General Strengths

- People and team oriented; communicate easily and build rapport with others
- Verbally persuasive
- Ability to have fun and use humor when interacting
- Creative; good at brainstorming ideas
- Good people skills that are used to inspire and influence others
- Optimistic and enthusiastic
- Ability to keep everyone motivated and inspired; expressive nature can be contagious

Sales Strengths

- Are optimistic and self-confident; verbally persuasive
- Meet people easily and are at ease with strangers
- Build rapport with buyers
- React enthusiastically to a buyer's situation
- Keep the pace lively when presenting and like to use strong visual support
- Provide incentives to encourage fast decisions from buyers

General Blind Spots
- Can have a tendency to oversell, overpromise, or exaggerate
- Can be verbose, overly wordy
- Use an approach that is too expressive and emotional for some styles
- Can be poor listeners; may interrupt or get sidetracked
- Can get bored easily; short attention span
- May be too trusting
- Overestimate ability to persuade others
- Can be impulsive; may not gather sufficient data when making decisions
- Can be poor with follow-through and inattentive to details
- Can have difficulty staying focused and managing time
- Are disorganized
- May have a fear of not being liked
- May abandon position in conflict; have trouble separating issues from individuals

Sales Blind Spots
- May not control time well; may run late
- Can be too trusting and take things at face value
- May overestimate the potential of a client
- May come across as overly optimistic or enthusiastic
- Can talk too much; may miss closing signals
- Can be uncomfortable with silence; will ask a probing question and may not remain silent long enough to hear the full answer
- May not present enough facts; may overpromise
- Can be careless with follow-through on smaller details

When you manage sales employees who exhibit high Impacting characteristics, then you will want to be sure to understand their preferred work environment motivators and the following tips for managing them.

Work Environment Motivators
- Opportunity to build relationships and work with people

- An environment that supports creativity and brainstorming
- Variety of tasks and activities
- Assignments that provide opportunity for recognition
- Freedom from detail
- Opportunity to verbalize
- Fun, energetic environment; positive team climate

Implications for Management
- Be informal and open; get to know them
- Provide recognition
- Assist with time management; set clear deadlines for completion of tasks
- Leverage their people skills
- Provide clear objectives and priorities
- Help with systems for organization
- Compliment on their people skills and creativity

Box 3: Supporting (Steadiness)

Individuals who show a high Supporting style tend to process more methodically and are focused on people. These people tend to be loyal, cooperative, calm, and methodical in how they deal with life. They are the team members who make sure that everyone on the team is doing okay. Security, stability, and sincere appreciation will likely motivate them.

Those with a strong Supporting style are often described as adaptable, systematic, unhurried, predictable, and consistent. Their needs-driven behavior is accommodation, and they also possess a need to be of help to others. When you communicate with individuals who exhibit high Supporting, you will want to be patient, draw out their opinions, provide a logical approach to the facts, relax and allow time for discussion, show how a solution would benefit them, clearly define all areas, and involve them in the planning stage.

When you receive communication from someone with a core Supporting style, it may appear nonemotional, indecisive, too indirect, and lacking in assertiveness. It may also seem as though the sender is providing an enormous amount of detail.

Supporting team members are loyal to those they identify with; they are good listeners, especially because they are patient and empathetic. High Supporting individuals are limited in that they tend to get in a rut, they resist change, and they hold grudges. They don't project a sense of urgency and are low risk takers.

If you are a Supporting type, to communicate more effectively you could improve your assertiveness skills, stop taking on the problems of others, and embrace change to help with communication.

Here is a summary of common strengths and areas to bring awareness to those who exhibit high Supporting characteristics.

General Strengths

- ◆ Systematic approach to tasks; systematic with follow-up
- ◆ People oriented; warm, friendly, and more subtle in their approach
- ◆ Calming and stabilizing team players
- ◆ Patient, cooperative, accommodating, and supportive of others
- ◆ Good listeners; ask questions
- ◆ Well prepared and thorough when communicating
- ◆ Good planners and organizers; plan ahead when change is necessary
- ◆ Ability to mask emotions; rarely rattled on the outside

Sales Strengths

- ◆ Respond well to leads generated by others
- ◆ Listen attentively and ask questions
- ◆ Act as buyer's advocate
- ◆ Deal with objections thoroughly and systematically
- ◆ Don't push or rush buyer
- ◆ Provide excellent service
- ◆ Provide systematic follow-up and keep accurate records

General Blind Spots

- Find it difficult to react quickly to changes and shifts in direction; may resist change
- Can be too indirect and hesitant to state their position
- Dislike confrontation, resulting in a tendency to tolerate conflict; can be slow to confront difficult relationships or people issues
- Tend to internalize their true feelings and not let others know where they stand on an issue
- Can be too accommodating and take on the problems of others
- Can take things or criticism personally
- Under pressure can have difficulty establishing priorities or getting started on new projects
- May lack a sense of urgency; too patient for results
- Have a tendency to see all sides of issues, and so decisions may not come easily

Sales Blind Spots

- Can be hesitant with cold calls
- Have a fear of coming on too strong, which can cause them to avoid asking the more penetrating questions
- Can be too reserved when an emotional appeal may work best
- May be too subtle; not as forceful as a situation calls for
- Are uncomfortable selling a new product until they have a complete understanding of the product and there is a proven track record
- May be too indirect and not push for close
- Tend to overservice
- May spend too much time in the office preparing

When you manage sales employees who exhibit high Supporting characteristics, then you will want to be sure to understand their preferred work environment motivators and the following tips for managing them.

Work Environment Motivators

◆ Predictability, security, and stability

◆ An environment that allows for closure

◆ Established procedures and processes to follow; well-defined boundaries

◆ Time to plan for changes

◆ Team approach to problem solving

◆ Long-term relationships with team members and customers

◆ Harmony with team members

◆ Supportive team climate

Implications for Management

◆ Provide information when delegating a new assignment; allow time for questions

◆ Patiently draw out their thoughts and opinions

◆ Don't rush them in the decision-making process

◆ Capitalize on their ability to develop organizational systems

◆ Prepare them in advance for change whenever possible

◆ Communicate regularly and thoroughly

◆ Compliment on their dependability, follow-through, and supportiveness

Box 4: Contemplating (Conscientiousness)

Individuals who show a high Contemplating style tend to process more methodically and are focused on tasks. These people tend to be analytical and precise. They value quality and accuracy on a project. They are the team members who keep standards high and pay attention to details. Professional standards, defined expectations, and a quality focus will likely motivate them.

These are the rule followers. Individuals high in Contemplating are painstaking, wary, meticulous, quality conscious, and perfectionistic. Their two primary driving forces are following the rules and complying with their own high standards.

To successfully communicate with high Contemplating types, use data and facts, and examine the argument from all sides. Keep on the task—don't socialize. If your opinion differs from that of a high Contemplating individual, disagree with the facts, not the person. These individuals will be best satisfied if you focus on quality by avoiding new solutions and sticking with proven ideas.

When receiving information from individuals high in Contemplating, it could seem excessive. They tend to appear as perfectionists, coming across as aloof, too rule focused, critical, and slow to proceed; bear with them. They must process the information before being able to communicate their ideas. High Contemplating individuals give their best to the team in the areas of critical thinking. However, they hesitate to act without precedent and are bound by procedures. Typically, they do not take risks or verbalize feelings, and they avoid controversy.

If you feel you fall into the Contemplating style, consider improving your patience, building more rapport, allowing more gray area, and being more accepting of differences.

Here is a summary of common strengths and areas to bring awareness to those who exhibit high Contemplating characteristics.

Strengths
- Very prepared and organized; thrive on order and structure
- Analytical, precise, accurate, and attentive to detail
- Thorough follow-up and follow-through
- Nonemotional approach to decision making
- Careful in making decisions; gather and focus on data and facts
- Thorough in following rules and procedures
- High standards for quality; tendency toward perfectionism

Sales Strengths
- Research market before contacting prospective customers
- Arrive on time and are well prepared and organized
- Ask detailed, exploring questions

- Are thorough and accurate; very thorough with follow-through
- Anticipate objections and are prepared with an answer; present data to overcome objections
- Allow buyers time to think

General Blind Spots
- Tend to overanalyze; lose sight of big picture
- Have difficulty making timely decisions; can get bogged down in details
- Can be too much of a perfectionist; may not know when to quit editing, refining, reviewing, etc.
- Tend to worry; fear of mistakes creates time-consuming tasks
- Are nitpicky or critical; may focus too much on negative versus positive
- Can be too critical of others; can be too hard on themselves
- Can become defensive when challenged or criticized
- Have difficulty with risk; will take risks only after knowing all the facts
- May overfocus on operational, task-oriented items
- Are slow to embrace change and new methods and ideas

Sales Blind Spots
- Can spend too much time researching and analyzing when qualifying; can be overkill
- May be too formal and reserved when an emotional appeal will work best
- Can ask too many questions; questions may come across as intense
- May provide too many details and facts, which can confuse buyers
- May hesitate to ask for close
- Can struggle with being flexible when presenting; may miss buying signals until they have completed their entire presentation

◆ Tendency to get stuck in overservicing

When you manage sales employees who exhibit high Contemplating characteristics, then you will want to be sure to understand their preferred work environment motivators and the following tips for managing them.

Work Environment Motivators
◆ Exact job description with clear standards
◆ Tasks that require precision and attention to detail
◆ Established rules, policies, and procedures
◆ An environment that supports time to analyze before making decisions
◆ Emphasis on quality over quantity
◆ Controlled work environment; no sudden changes

Implications for Management
◆ Provide complete instructions on assignments
◆ Clearly define expectations
◆ Leverage their ability to define standards and procedures
◆ Respect their need for privacy; don't get too personal too soon
◆ Communicate in detail
◆ Allow time to think and analyze; don't rush decision making
◆ Compliment on the precision, accuracy, and quality

COMMUNICATION PREFERENCES

Table 10-2 shows in more detail how the key behavioral styles prefer to receive communication and can help people in sales to cue in on others' behavioral styles so they both initiate contact and respond in a way that will enhance communication.

When we are aware of how the different styles respond to verbal and nonverbal communication, we have a better chance of being successful. Table 10-2 gives you important pointers on how to communicate via e-mail, written proposals, and verbal presentations to make a successful sale.

Communication Styles			
	E-Mail	**Proposals**	**Presentations**
Driving	◆ Use bullets ◆ Be brief ◆ Focus on results and benefits	◆ Use bullets ◆ Highlight benefits ◆ Summarize bottom-line results	◆ Be fast ◆ Focus on business results
Impacting	◆ Use positive introduction ◆ Highlight benefits and generate excitement	◆ Use colorful visuals ◆ Bring sample if appropriate ◆ Summarize benefits to people	◆ Be friendly and positive ◆ Break the ice ◆ Be brief and fast
Supporting	◆ Use friendly introduction ◆ Outline service or product in a step-by-step process	◆ Outline products and services in detail ◆ Attach supporting materials if possible ◆ Include references	◆ Be friendly and sincere ◆ Leave time for review ◆ Use team language
Contemplating	◆ Use formal approach ◆ Get right to the point ◆ Attach details	◆ Be accurate and detailed ◆ Provide statistics or research about products and services	◆ Be formal and courteous ◆ Be accurate ◆ Use graphs and charts

Table 10-2. Behavioral preferences and communication styles

PEOPLE-READING SIGNS

One of the most valuable skills your salespeople can learn is how to read their prospects' behavioral style. People rarely share their results with acquaintances, let alone with complete strangers, so the only way salespeople can know how to adapt their communication styles is by observing the communication style in others. Beware, however, that when observing behavior, you may be seeing a "mask." Act on what you observe, but watch closely and pay attention to how your communications are received. The following cues will help you determine a person's preferred communication style.

Driving
- Decides quickly
- Takes action
- Moves quickly
- Takes charge
- Goes first
- Takes bold, often aggressive action
- Gets right to the point
- Tells others what to do
- Expresses concern for the bottom line

Impacting
- Starts conversations easily and readily
- Is fun to be with
- Expresses optimism
- Makes friends easily
- Is generally outgoing
- Persuades others

Supporting
- Follows orders
- Avoids causing problems
- Avoids arguments
- Listens patiently
- Demonstrates understanding of others' feelings
- Relates to others warmly
- Rarely makes demands of others
- Is easy to get along with
- Is a "nice person"

Contemplating

- Has a place for everything, everything in its place
- Is careful, perhaps guarded, when speaking
- Thinks things through
- Is not impulsive
- Is a stickler for quality
- Writes detailed reports and memos
- Plans ahead
- Seems to want to work alone

REVIEWING SALES ONLINE DISC PROFILE RESULTS

Before a manager talks to an employee about his or her DISC assessment results, be sure to review the following guidelines. Too often employees get the impression that there are right and wrong behavior styles, when the intention is to help employees be more effective by using what comes naturally to their best advantage and adapting to other styles in ways that might not come intuitively.

When reviewing a DISC behavior profile, explain that:

- DISC is a tool that measures observable human behavior and emotion.
- Behavioral styles can provide information about how an individual makes decisions—in other words, the person's preferred process and approach.
- DISC does not measure personality, as personality takes into account everything that we are and not the behavior we exhibit.
- There are no good or bad profiles.

   Review the four DISC factors:

- D stands for Driving and measures how individuals respond to **problems.**
- I stands for Impacting and measures how individuals interact with and influence **people.**
- S stands for Supporting and measures the **pace** of the environment that individuals prefer.

♦ C stands for Contemplating and measures how individuals respond to **procedures** and rules set by others.

BEHAVIOR PROFILE CASE STUDY AND INTERPRETATION

Jill's manager is reviewing her behavioral profile, which shows the results from her DISC assessment, the one she took when the company hired her. She is now in her first six months with the organization and is performing well as a district sales representative. Her manager wants to provide Jill with support and training that will strengthen her sales skills. He also knows that there might be considerations for retaining her, to help her to stay satisfied in her job.

As the graph in Figure 10-1 shows, Jill's preferred style—her natural style—is Impacting. Her score of 97 percent shows that she will be very outgoing, social, and people oriented.

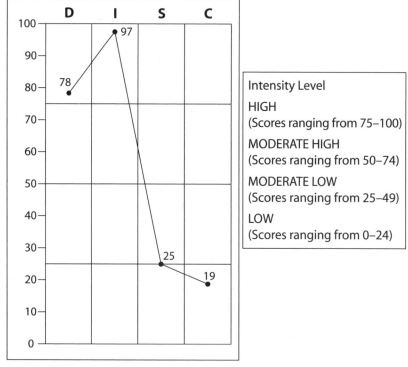

Figure 10-1. Jill's behavioral profile

These attributes will make it easier for someone in sales, whose success relies on talking frequently with prospects and customers to engage them in conversation, explore their needs, and establish rapport. Individuals with this style tend to be optimistic and enthusiastic and are motivated by recognition. Jill has recently closed a deal, and her manager makes a note to publicly recognize her success at the next sales meeting. People who score high in Impacting tend to be trusting of others and build relationships easily.

Her second highest style is Driving (78 percent), indicating that she will exhibit a sense of urgency and drive toward results. Combined with the high Impacting score, it shows that she will use her people skills to achieve those results.

Jill scores low (25 percent) in the Supporting style, indicating that she prefers less structure and an environment that is fast moving and allows for variety and change. Her manager needs to be aware of these preferences, as they will contribute strongly to her job satisfaction. Where possible, he should adapt his management style to allow her freedom to operate while keeping her accountable for meeting her goals. He will check in to be sure there continues to be enough variety in her job.

She also scores low (19 percent) in the Contemplating factor, indicating she likes to operate independently and prefers less restrictive rules and looser constraints.

Based on these results, here are some potential overextensions for Jill's preferred style:

◆ Can lack attention to detail
◆ May break the rules and ask for forgiveness later
◆ Can be impatient when people move too slowly or when results come too slowly
◆ Can be too quick to trust
◆ Can be perceived as being overly optimistic
◆ Can have a tendency to work without a structured plan and may take on too much at once

There is a wealth of information for managing your sales employees to help them be more successful and happier in their jobs. Being aware of the possible shortcomings should help Jill's manager be more vigilant and ready to provide coaching to protect her from these pitfalls.

Preferred vs. Expressed Style

Another aspect of DISC profiling explains why it can be difficult to read style preferences by observing people. We all have our innate style preferences, our natural behavioral tendencies—this is our *preferred* style. As we grow and experience new environments, we tend to adapt to be more successful in our work. We call the adaptive style our *expressed* style.

It's helpful to assess both the preferred and expressed styles so you can see what is truly preferred and where someone has adapted. The preferred style will give you insight into the preferred style for being managed as well as preferred job characteristics. By comparing the expressed style, you can see where employees may be adapting their style to meet the demands of the work environment. However, under stress, an individual will revert back to the behavior in his or her preferred or natural style.

Using the results from the DISC profile will help salespeople become more aware of how they can adapt their styles for job success. Managers will have greater insight into how they can support and develop employees to improve their job skill fit. They will also be able to improve job satisfaction.

SALES TEAM BEHAVIORS ANALYSIS

In addition to their use for individual development, looking at a sales team as a whole can provide valuable information to create a more effective team.

Team Quadrant Analysis

The team quadrant is used for team building and presents eight individual categories team behavior (see Chapter 7, pages

94–95 to review the team quadrant descriptors). The team quadrant displays the various roles each team member contributes to the team. Team members are placed on the quadrant based on their preferred style scores.

The team quadrant can be used for the following:

- To identify the behavioral strengths and tendencies that each team member contributes to the team.
- To identify team members' behavioral blind spots or overextensions that can impact team performance.
- To provide insight into potential communication conflict or challenges to enhance working relationships and enhance team effectiveness.
- To identify behavioral gaps. If there are empty segments on a team quadrant, this can help to identify roles that are important to a team but are not currently represented on the team.

Having both individual results for development and group results for team analysis is an example of multiple uses for the same data. Using assessments that gather information and provide multiple applications is a more efficient use of time and investment. Thinking styles offer another way that we've discovered to collect data for development purposes and apply those data in new ways.

THINKING-STYLES ASSESSMENT

You might have already stumbled across learning styles at some time in your career (auditory, visual, and kinesthetic learners). All these propensities, or preferences, for a way of communication or learning help us to adapt, appreciate other styles, and compensate both as managers and as individuals. While conducting our research on new ways to assess the sales candidates, we looked at the data we were collecting on candidates during the assessment and found that we could identify some other attributes that would help in developing employees after hiring. We were looking to provide information that would parallel the critical thinking component, which shows how a person reasons. You can't use critical thinking for development because it's a measure of intelligence (and you can't change a person's level of intelligence).

So we thought about how we could group the competencies to determine how a person processes data. That resulted in the measurement we call thinking styles. Not only can we measure thinking styles, but we can also tie them to job preferences, which means that a person's thinking-style preferences can help identify areas to develop and improve performance.

Thinking style determines the degree to which individuals prefer thinking about decisions and problems in a particular way. It reflects how individuals gather and process information, how they use that information, and what types of information they gravitate toward. It describes how an individual's thought process helps the person to analyze problems, evaluate information, and form opinions based on patterns and preferences, as well as to remember and use information. Analyzing people's thinking styles offers another way to understand how individuals naturally approach a work situation. Looking in detail at how someone gathers and processes information provides a window into what will be easier or more difficult in relation to a specific work environment.

The thinking-style dimensions, however, are not measures of intelligence or cognitive ability. The thinking style reflects how an individual processes information, whereas cognitive ability reflects aptitude or a general level of intelligence. That's why determining and analyzing an individual's thinking style will be helpful when developing employees. It's another way to understand strengths and areas to develop in relation to the demands of a specific work environment or situation. It also helps in retaining employees by understanding their work environment preferences.

Understanding an individual's thinking style explains how an individual approaches and completes vital tasks. Use this information to manage and motivate employees.

HISTORY OF THE THINKING STYLE
Cognitive-Style Theory

Samuel Messick was an American professor of psychology and a leader in the field of educational testing. In the 1980s, Messick's research indicated that cognitive styles are propensities to think about information, solve problems, and make judgments. Cognitive styles reflect patterns of how people take in and process information. As Messick observed, cognitive styles differ from intellectual or cognitive abilities in a number of ways.

- Cognitive abilities refer to the content of cognition or the question of *what*. What kind of information is being processed by what operation and in what form?
- Cognitive styles, in contrast, consider the question of *how*. How or in what manner do individuals process information?

Cognitive style incorporates personality, interpersonal, and competency aspects. Cognitive style indicates that individuals differ in how they prefer to solve problems and interact while making decisions.

Cognitive (thinking) styles describe how individuals prefer to perceive, organize, analyze, and recall information and create the backbone for how individuals think and solve problems.

THINKING-STYLE PROFILE

The best method to determine individuals' thinking styles is through their answers to work-related competency questions. Based on their rankings of these competencies demonstrated in their past experience, their answers can show how they prefer to evaluate information as it is applied in a goal-directed manner within a work setting.

For development purposes, individuals can build their competencies in all the thinking styles through training to expand their ability in areas of weakness. As with competencies, there are associated behaviors that can be observed to measure progress in an area.

THE THREE THINKING STYLES

Through state-of-the-art research and validation, we have defined three predominant thinking styles. Here's an overview of the three styles.

Analytical

The analytical thinking style is a data-driven approach to problem solving and processing information, where the individual focuses in the present, grounded in the here and now. Within the workplace, a person with a preference for analytical thinking will consider financial information and the immediate effects on profitability when making decisions and solving problems. In the sales environment, someone with this preference is more likely to focus on the numbers and will be more concerned with profitability. For example, suppose a customer is weighing two product solutions to solve an important product fulfillment capability. One program, available now, solves much of the problem, but not all of it. The other program, an entirely new application, solves the problem completely but isn't available for six months. Someone who approaches the sales solution from an analytical perspective will focus on the bottom line and the number rather than which solution might help develop a long-term relationship or opportunities for future sales. The analytical thinker, focused on the bottom line, will close the immediate deal, the short-term solution.

Strategic

The strategic thinking style is a long-term approach to problem solving and information processing, grounded in taking ideas and making them workable. Within the workplace, a person who prefers strategic thinking will consider the big-picture and holistic issues in making decisions and solving problems.

So to continue with the same sales situation, let's elaborate and say the customer is weighing two computer software products, one is available now and will yield short-term sales dollars. But the software only partially solves the customer's problem and will take precious time for staff to install and adopt. The strategic salesperson knows that a new software application coming in the next six months will fulfill all the customer's needs. The strategic thinker knows that the customer would prefer to wait, given all the facts, and so opts for determining the best solution for both the customer and the selling company. Selling the long-term solution makes the most sense for long-term customer satisfaction and the resulting goodwill, rather than a quick buck and limited future opportunities.

Innovative

The innovative thinking style is a curiosity-driven approach to problem solving and information processing that focuses on using information to generate new ideas. Within the workplace, a person who prefers innovative thinking will use brainstorming and consider new solutions, ideas, and opportunities in making decisions and solving problems.

In the sales environment we've described, the innovative thinker will explore many options, review different approaches, and present new possible solutions rather than the two given choices that appear to be the only ones available to the customer. An alternative solution might couple services to support implementing the short-term product and converting to the new software when it's available. Another possibility is to lease the software running on remote servers with an option to install the new product when it's available. A third solution might be to outsource the entire function until the software is available.

Analyzing thinking styles isn't always as simplistic as the software sales solution case presents. There are always degrees of style preference. When selecting an assessment for measuring thinking styles, you will want to be able to compare preferences with others in the sales position and determine which are most important and what effect the strengths or weakness in any style will have on performance and job satisfaction.

When assessing thinking styles, you will want results that tell you whether:

- The style will drive behavior in most to all situations.
- The style may be important in some situations but not in others.
- The style is not a strong driver of an individual's behavior.

THINKING-STYLES CASE STUDY

John Smith is a sales representative working in a financial institution, and his manager is looking at results that show his thinking style. Figure 10-2 presents his scores for the three thinking styles.

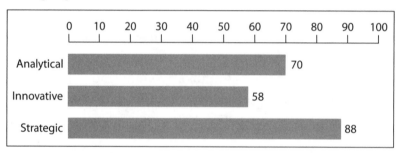

Figure 10-. A graph of John Smith's thinking styles

Thinking-Styles Interpretation

John Smith's strongest thinking style is strategic, which scores in the high range (88). This indicates that he has a strong tendency to focus on strategic issues when making decisions and will be able to develop a clear strategy and the actions necessary in order to complete his objectives. The analytical style scores in the medium range, indicating that he will focus on financial and profitability aspects when making decisions. He scores lowest in the innovative style (although the score is in the medium range), and so he will be less focused on looking for innovative solutions and opportunities when making decisions but instead will fall back on the same stock choices he employs in similar situations. He is less likely to sell add-ons to the stock offerings or identify new opportunities for combining products and services. Consequently, a manager could work with him to show different ways to consider innovative alternatives.

Thinking styles help to develop employees in ways that will increase their productivity. In addition, helping your salespeople be more successful will contribute to their long-term job satisfaction. Using the development data to analyze your sales teams will help you create a more rewarding environment and more proficient teams.

MOVING FORWARD

The "one style fits all" approach is not an effective way to coach and manage your sales team. Learning about their behavioral style will help you understand what drives and motivates your sales staff, how they prefer to approach problem-solving and working with data, as well as their communication style. Behavioral data can help you to learn:

- An individual's strengths
- Potential blind spots
- Motivational environmental factors

As difficult as it can be to find top talent, the challenge of retaining the best can be even harder. The next chapter shows you in greater detail how to apply what you've learned for retaining your top salespeople. Through a case study, you'll see how to directly apply development assessment results to retain a valued salesperson.

Chapter

11 Applying What You Know So Your Top Salespeople Stay

Do not follow where the path may lead. Go instead where there is no path and leave a trail.

—Harold R. McAlindon
Little Book of Big Ideas

MANY BUSINESS LEADERS ACKNOWLEDGE HOW THEY ARE CHALLENGED IN FINDING and recruiting premier salespeople. They say it's also hard to keep them once they've been on the job for a while. Top performers are tough negotiators, and they know their market value. If you've effectively screened and hired top performers, they are likely to produce a significant return on your investment. Losing them can be costly. Regardless of the economic landscape, up or down, good salespeople have many options in the business world that are being presented to them on a regular basis. They also like new experiences. So they tend to be open to new possibilities in the job market.

Beyond retaining high-performing salespeople, you want them to be satisfied employees. That doesn't mean they're complacent, because more often your top talent who rate their job satisfaction as high also prefer to feel challenged.

The retention game has changed in the 21st century; what made top sales talent stay in a job 10 to 20 years ago won't necessarily prompt them to stay at your company today. Research conducted by Kaye and Jordan-Evans shows that the following opportunities actually made high performers stay. Their findings were ranked in order of preference.

1. Exciting work and challenges
2. Career growth, learning, and development
3. Great people
4. Fair pay
5. Good boss
6. Recognition and valued respect
7. Benefits
8. Meaningful work and opportunity to make a difference
9. Pride in organization, mission, and its products and services
10. Great work environment and culture

Excelling in all these areas in your company is a challenge, and yet doing so is essential, as noted by many top executive leaders. The 2009 Job Satisfaction Survey conducted by the Society for Human Resources Management states in the executive summary that having opportunities to use one's skills and talents was among the top five most important contributors to employee job satisfaction.

We know that creating an environment that encourages people to stay won't happen without paying attention to what matters most to your salespeople. Just as companies need to make it a priority to be hiring ready, they should also make retaining high-performance employees a priority. Managers need to know what will make their people stay.

MOTIVATING OR SELF-MOTIVATING

I often say that you cannot motivate someone. When I speak in front of a group and say that, the managers often challenge me. "What do you mean?" they ask. "That's my job. What do you mean I can't motivate someone?" My reply is that you cannot motivate someone else, because ultimately all people are self-motivated. And self-motivation is often more apparent in high-performance sales-

> **Tip for Retaining Top Talent**
> One of the chief ingredients for retaining your top talent is to create an environment where they feel self-motivated.

people than in other employees.

Managers then ask, "If you can't motivate someone, what can you do?" What you can do is hold people accountable. People are motivated to do what they want to do, not what you want them to do. So a lot of time gets wasted trying to manage your salespeople by attempting to motivate them, something that is quite impossible to do.

A salesperson's boss, as a manager, is the one with the most influence to create that environment and control the day-to-day climate. Here are some of the basics for creating a self-motivating environment for your salespeople.

Practice the Platinum Rule
Go beyond the Golden Rule. Don't treat people the way you want to be treated; treat them the way they want to be treated.

The members of your sales force are different from one another. Don't force them to fit a mold. Don't make assumptions about what environment they prefer to operate in; this is why assessment is so important. Take time to ask your salespeople what they want, how they prefer to communicate, which rewards mean the most to them, and what their aspirations are. Reviewing their development assessment and creating a development plan provides an excellent opportunity to review what is most important to them without judging. Listen to their answers so you can adapt to their behavioral preferences and understand their values and aspirations.

Teach Your Business to Your High-Potential Salespeople
When salespeople are very goal driven, they will do best and be most content when they understand how their actions

impact the overall success of the business. This principle will take them beyond just doing their job.

Constantly communicate your mission and vision and make sure your salespeople know where they fit into that mission and vision. Be sure they understand what brand image you want to convey for your organization. Open your books and be willing to talk specifics about the direction your company is going. Give them the decision-making chain of command and any other information that's helpful for removing impediments to their success. By understanding the big picture, they'll be more motivated to help take your company where you want to go. You'll also develop trust that encourages them to exercise their freedom to succeed in ways that support the organization's goals.

Communicate Clearly and Frequently

When left without clear direction, motivated people tend to go in their own preferred way. So don't assume even your top sales talent knows what is expected of them. Use the tools described in the chapters on hiring and developing to clearly outline job responsibilities; use measurements for performance reviews. Employees will take initiative even if not told what's expected of them. Defining expectations up front will reduce frustration for both you and your salespeople. Determine how much you can communicate through e-mail and over the telephone vs. having meetings face-to-face, how often you need to hold team meetings vs. seeing individuals one-on-one.

When you communicate what the organization wishes to accomplish in a listening environment, in addition to being a motivator for your salespeople, you can reap amazing benefits. Products that are differentiated or have a distinct advantage over the competition are easier to sell. Listening to those who are closest to your customers can be revealing. The result is the motivation of feeling listened to, participating in the success of the company, and producing products that beat the competition. Similarly, surfacing other factors such as supply chain problems, faster pricing decisions, or a wider variety of packaging solutions that contribute to the sales cycle running more smoothly can contribute to a more motivating environment.

Get to Know Your Salespeople as More Than Employees

There should never be an instance where you approach one of your salespeople in the hallway and think "Oh ... what is her name again?" Salespeople want to know that they are making a difference. They want others in the organization to know who they are and what they are contributing.

Not only do you want to make sure you know every one of your high-performing salespeople by name and recognize their contributions publicly, it also pays to get to know them outside the office. You'd be amazed at what insights their "alter egos" can provide. By taking time to establish relationships with them that go deeper than just manager–employee, you can learn what makes them tick and you can pick up information that will help you create the work atmosphere that fits them best and perhaps pave the way for others to follow in their path to success.

Leverage the Power of a Buddy System

Use those high-performing salespeople who already work for you to mentor your new hires. Such a mentoring program is a great way to introduce people to your organization. Having mentors gives your new hires a safe way to ask confidential questions, look beyond written policy and procedure manuals, and find their place within your organization much more quickly than if left to fly solo.

Keep the Work Environment Up to Date

Give your salespeople the up-to-date tools they need to help them operate efficiently. They will interpret their value by the tools they receive to do their job. Make sure they can see the benefits and receive the support and training they need to be effective with any new technology; otherwise they'll never use it.

Keep the workplace up to date and fresh. Encourage people to refresh their office space regularly. Sometimes moving offices helps people start anew and gives them a reason to clean up and throw out what's obsolete. A tired environment will affect performance negatively; a vibrant environment will invigorate.

Have Fun at Work!

When you incorporate fun and creativity in the workplace, you build an atmosphere in which innovation flows freely. Create a learning environment for sales training that goes beyond PowerPoint presentations. Take field trips. Feed into their competitive nature. Provide a room filled with toys they can play with (video games are usually a *big* hit). After all, have you ever heard of an employee leaving a job that was fun and paid well? Make sure these activities are directly tied to the results your salespeople are trying to achieve.

Conduct Exit Interviews

If you do lose a top salesperson, you definitely want to know why. Conducting an exit interview will provide you with valuable information that may help you overcome problems others are encountering in your organization. Be prepared for directness when you conduct this discussion. Do not be defensive about the information you hear. Instead, focus on what you can learn that will help in the future.

REWARDING YOUR HIGH-PERFORMING SALESPEOPLE

When you understand what motivates your salespeople, you'll realize that not all employees want to be rewarded the same way. For some, a public announcement is excruciatingly painful, while others would say, "Don't bother if it's going to be kept a secret" (meaning blast it out to everyone in the organization). Knowing what rewards are valued and knowing how to present them are equally important for creating an environment where top performers will want to stay.

Prestige, Position, and Title

All employees want to feel valued. For some it is their status that makes them feel appreciated. When you see certifications, certificates, and diplomas and other symbols that represent prestige hanging on the employees' walls, you know they like to display their position, credentials, and title. They feel valued, important. Others could do without that kind of recognition. It is not that important to them. Having a prestigious title, however, such as adding the word "senior" to indicate a promotion, can be a big motivator.

Popularity and Recognition

Most salespeople want to be liked. This could mean liked in terms of respect, and it could mean liked socially by other people. There is a difference. Some people in sales don't care so much about being liked; they care about respect.

Others want to shine in public. They want their names to appear somewhere that's public. They want visibility, they want recognition, and they like it publicly. They want everyone to know about their achievements. Some people are not as comfortable receiving public recognition. They prefer recognition one-on-one.

Monetary Rewards

Many people think in terms of value. They see themselves as having value, and they want to be rewarded monetarily based on that value. So they use monetary rewards as a yardstick measure. For the highly competitive, these rewards are part of their self-motivation.

Consequently, it's important to have an evaluation system in place. How often are you evaluating and measuring performance? You also need to know how closely individuals tie monetary rewards to their motivation, and you need to know the extent to which the rewards are on par with people's expectations and with where they believe they should be.

CREATING A MOTIVATING WORK ENVIRONMENT FOR LEE

In Chapter 6, we learned about Lee Washington as he was a candidate and again in Chapter 8, which focused on a development plan for Lee based on his candidate report. Let's look further into what the report tells us that will be useful for managing Lee day to day and for ensuring that his manager creates a motivating environment for him.

In Lee's behavioral assessment, he scored high in Impact and Driving. We know that Lee is people focused, prefers to communicate verbally to establish relationships, and wants quick responses rather than detailed reports. He's also a big-idea person and is less concerned with details and implementation. With low scores in Contemplating and Support, he likes variety and change and the freedom to operate independently. His primary values indicate that he is goal driven and will be motivated by achieving challenging goals. In addition, he values recognition for his authority and ability to influence others. While Lee's behavioral profile is typical of many who are successful in sales, it's a sure bet that others in your organization will have a different behavioral profile. Again, that's why having an assessment is so helpful and prevents managers from operating on false assumptions.

By starting with development when first bringing new hires on board, you are taking advantage of the enthusiasm with which new employees arrive. You immediately open the channels of communication and establish a listening environment. When you use a behavioral assessment, you uncover the individual's preferred communication style. Many who go into sales describe themselves as a "people person." Yet with his high Driving score, Lee will want you to be direct, without a lot of detail or socializing.

To accommodate Lee's behavioral style, which is very typical of goal-oriented salespeople, his manager can adapt the following ways to create an optimal environment.

Availability of New Opportunities and Challenges

Lee is driven. As soon as he is oriented and ready to assume the responsibility, put him in charge of a new project or give him the task of creating one. Make sure that you have another new project waiting for him once his current project ends. This will continue to fuel him and prevent boredom from setting in. Being in charge of new projects will fulfill Lee's need for challenges, creativity, and recognition as an authority.

Opportunity to Advance

Lee has already demonstrated in his career that he thrives on growth opportunities and looks for jobs where he can continually advance his position. Individuals like Lee get bored easily, and so it's important to create a development plan for him to continually move forward in his career. Identify Lee's talents, skills, and interests. Discuss with him the experience, the behaviors, and the results he needs to help him grow within your department or organization. Then create jobs and career paths that keep him challenged.

Freedom to Operate Creatively

Because Lee is goal driven, achievement is a motivating factor. He will thrive in an environment where he has freedom to operate. He will likely achieve more if he sets sales goals for himself rather than having measures imposed by his manager. He will thrive where there is little structure around how something needs to get accomplished. In the case where you require some structure, give him options about how he can achieve a goal.

Lee is motivated by developing the big-picture idea. He tends to think in broader views and will serve you and your organization best if he is driving and executing his plan. Don't restrict him. Give him the flexibility and creative freedom to innovate. Hold him accountable for results rather than the methods he chooses to achieve them.

For people like Lee, the freedom to choose how they accomplish their goals will often result in new ways—faster, more efficient, higher quality—of getting things done.

A Feeling of Adding Value

From his core values, it's clear Lee will feel valued if you make sure he has worthwhile work to do, where he can be an authority and contribute substantially to the outcome. Lee will want to feel a sense of accomplishment—a sense that he is really contributing. One way is to make him an expert in a specific area and then ask him to bring that knowledge to the sales team. He will thrive with a growth plan that provides him with new challenges, chances to learn new skills, and opportunities to lead. This is a surefire way to make Lee feel he is a valued member of the organization.

Freedom to Lead

Lee likes to be the authority. He likes to lead and direct. When involved in a project with a team, he will be inspired by influencing others on the team. As a new hire, if Lee is not ready to take the lead, he'll be satisfied to know the opportunity is there for advancement, at least for a while.

Recognition of Achievements and Contributions

Lee enjoys being told that he has done exceptional work. He likes to feel as though he is leading the pack. This is in part due to his ego drive and in part because of his competitive nature. The fact that employee recognition is a strong part of the company culture is important to Lee.

To keep your high-performance salespeople satisfied, it's equally important to understand that rewards don't always mean financial compensation, that there are different kinds of rewards, and that different individuals prefer to be recognized in different ways. Using assessment results to treat your salespeople as individuals and tailor a motivating environment will go far toward making them more successful. In the end, the organization will reap the rewards.

High-performing salespeople simply don't leave jobs where they feel challenged, have exciting work to do, are rewarded fairly, and feel their contributions matter. Having the right tools and objective data to assist managers will go a long way toward creating an environment that attracts and retains high-performing salespeople.

MOVING FORWARD

Once you've found the perfect fit, that is, the right salespeople in the right jobs, keeping them motivated and wanting to stay in the job will require the same dedication to a process as hiring and developing them. Making retention a core focus for your top talent will reinforce your hiring and development investment. Assessments can provide a wealth of information to help managers identify the best ways to recognize and reward individuals. Using best practices for retaining your top talent in a way that recognizes the salespeople's preferred styles, areas of strength, and motivating environments will challenge and keep them motivated.

Afterword:
The Solution

THE TIME IS RIGHT FOR TAKING A LONG, HARD LOOK AT INVESTING IN SELECTION. As
the economy recovers, pressure on the current workforce to
meet the needs of growing demands is sure to follow. At the
same time, many people are applying for jobs that don't suit
them. Creating a hiring strategy and allocating resources
might, at first glance, appear as a cost to an organization.
However, the long-term benefits associated with the implementation of a selection system make it a sound investment.
You'll find the right sales talent, help them hit the ground running with easy integration into your organization, and provide
the right support and ongoing development to excel so they'll
want to stay.

In the absence of a hiring strategy and a selection system,
organizations tend to rely primarily on résumé screening and
applicant performance in an interview. The interview process is
often an unstructured, loose discussion focusing more on personality than important, job-related information. Research indicates that strong performance in an unstructured interview
doesn't effectively predict strong performance on the job.

Candidates are often measured on their ability to make a good impression. For example, extroverts may engage others quickly and be charming without having the critical thinking needed for long-term success.

A failure to focus on position-specific factors often results in selection of employees ill-equipped to perform successfully on the job. These are the poor performers that become so difficult and time consuming for managers. Some issues likely to arise include an inability to understand and apply training in a timely manner and a tendency to become dependent on others to get the job done right. A recent study showed that organizations that fail to address these issues quickly and astutely are likely to struggle due to poor performance and mismanagement of human capital. In a survey of 700 executive managers in the United States, they found that each manager loses an average of 34 days a year managing poor performers—employees who are not meeting the established performance standards of the organization. This translates to approximately one hour a day for each manager, or 12 percent of their time! Imagine how much more productive these managers could be if they didn't have to worry about poor performers. Finding a way to establish that an applicant possesses the knowledge, skills and experience necessary for the job is a much more effective use of time and resources.

Creating a process that effectively predicts applicant performance follows a simple, straightforward process that makes intuitive sense. The process begins with a thorough job analysis that leverages persons from the target group who are expert in the expectations and demands associated with the position. The focus is on capturing the essential knowledge, skills, and abilities necessary for success. The gathered information is categorized into simple, well-defined areas, or competencies, necessary for success in the job.

The best companies focus on building a strong culture that is part of its brand—Southwest Airlines and Starbucks are examples. This selection for culture often involves them matching on values. When employee values match the company's values, retention and engagement are significantly higher. The most successful organizations hire employees who look forward to coming to work.

A behaviorally focused, structured interview is another key component. Having relevant behavioral interview guides to augment selection testing is a key to involving hiring managers in a meaningful way. In these interviews, relevant experience and other softer skills (core values, work style, personality) can be assessed. The testing portion of the selection process narrows the interview pool and allows for selecting the best candidates among a pool of well-qualified people.

If you haven't used assessments or discover in reading this book those you are using are limited in what they provide, then I encourage you to find companies that offer trial assessments, and take advantage of trying them out and review the results. I invite you to contact XBInsight to request a complimentary profile and receive feedback. Assess a sales candidate; try it out.

If you're stuck on how to begin implementing this, here are some first steps you can take. Any one of these will have immediate benefits. Start by creating performance standards for the existing positions. You will see how your salespeople are spending their time. During your next candidate interview, use the competency and values interviewing questions we've provided; try them out.

My wish is that you will be a hiring-ready company that attracts top sales performers and that you create an environment that keeps them, so you have the sales talent you need to grow and thrive in business.

Appendix

Definition of Terms and Frequently Asked Questions

TERMS

Personnel assessment A systematic and comprehensive process of evaluating a candidate's knowledge, skills, and abilities. The critical objective is to identify the candidate's current capabilities and potential to perform successfully within the role. Personnel assessment is used for:

- ◆ Selection
- ◆ Development
- ◆ Promotion
- ◆ Succession planning

Personnel assessment tool Any test or procedure (for example, ability test, structured interview, or work sample) used to measure an individual's employment or career-related qualifications and interests.

Reliability The extent to which an assessment tool is consistent or free from random error in measurement.

Validity The extent to which an assessment tool measures what it is intended to measure.

Cognitive testing This involves the use of pencil and paper tasks to assess a wide range of abilities, including attention, memory, problem-solving, language skills, and intellectual functioning. It is the process of determining an individual's cognitive strengths and weaknesses from qualitative (approach to tasks and observed behavior) and quantitative (standardized and scaled measures) perspectives. Cognitive ability is considered by many researchers to be the single best predictor of both life and job performance outcomes (Herrnstein & Murray, 1994). Traditional cognitive ability assessments are widely used in personnel selection based on findings that they predict performance both on-the-job and in training (Schmidt & Hunter, 1998).

Uniform guidelines These guidelines incorporate a single set of principles that are designed to assist employers, labor organizations, employment agencies, and licensing and certification boards to comply with requirements of federal law prohibiting employment practices that discriminate on the grounds of race, color, religion, sex, and national origin. They are designed to provide a framework for determining the proper use of tests and other selection procedures.

FREQUENTLY ASKED QUESTIONS

How do I administer the testing?
All testing is administered online.

What does it mean to meet EEOC guidelines?
The EEOC guidelines provide the standards for the level of ethics in how tests should be used.

How do you measure productivity and retention?
You can measure productivity and retention by looking at each organization and each job to determine job outcomes. There are studies to determine the gaps in the organization's workforce and how companies differentiate themselves in their industries.

How is the assessment process customized to a particular job or organization?

The measures used to assess the relevant skills and characteristics are chosen based on a clear understanding of the critical job requirements. This requires completion of a job profile, review of current job descriptions, and discussions between the hiring manager and the assessor. From this, the assessment battery is tailored to the relevant position and the organizational environment.

The process allows for the identification of core competencies and other characteristics and leads to a customized job profile. It identifies the skills, abilities and other characteristics to look for in potential candidates for selection purposes.

Who conducts assessments?

Assessors should be members of the American Psychological Association (APA) or Society of Industrial/Organizational Psychology (SIOP) and have professional liability insurance. They also need to follow proper risk management and test handling policies, as required by the EEOC Uniform Guidelines on Employee Selection Procedures.

How does assessment work?

The assessment process consists of professionally developed and validated measures of personality and critical thinking. This process also often includes an in-depth interview, case study, and/or role-play.

After all measures have been completed, a trained professional integrates observations from the assessment with data collected to identify the strengths and developmental needs of the candidate. The results are provided both verbally and in a written report. The written report includes suggestions to enhance the strengths and/or to overcome limitations of the candidate.

Why is assessment important to business outcomes?

Assessment is not just about prediction. It is also about shaping the future through well-informed selection decisions, development, and organizational interventions. It is the most thorough approach available. Assessment can have a significant and beneficial impact on:

- Development of your employees
- Senior team collaboration and productivity
- Organizational culture
- Business strategy
- What is adverse impact?

Adverse impact is defined by the Uniform Guidelines as a *substantially different rate* of selection in hiring, promotion, or other employment decision that works to the disadvantage of members of a race, sex, or ethnic group (referred to as *Title VII*) and prohibits employment discrimination on the basis of race, color, religion, sex, or national origin. The *Equal Employment Opportunity Commission (EEOC)* is the federal agency responsible for enforcement of Title VII.

Why use competency assessments?
A competency is a cluster of related knowledge, skills, and attitudes that affects a major part of one's job (a role or responsibility) that correlates with performance on the job, that can be measured against well-accepted standards, and that can be improved via training and development.

Competency assessments can provide a valuable tool for employee development, coaching, and training. Some of the benefits of evaluating competencies for your sales team include:

- Aligning individual goals with company goals
- Providing individuals with focus on those areas that have the greatest impact on their overall effectiveness and performance
- Aligning development opportunities with the organization's requirements for success
- Providing a framework for ongoing coaching

Index
